CRYSTAL PAIN

GOD'S ETCHINGS THROUGH GRIEF,
THE PANDEMIC, AND SPIRITUAL WARFARE

CECILY C. WILLIAMS

Crystal Pain

Trilogy Christian Publishers A Wholly Owned Subsidiary of Trinity Broadcasting Network

2442 Michelle Drive Tustin, CA 92780

Copyright © 2023 by Cecily Williams

Scripture quotations marked AMPC are taken from the Amplified Bible, Copyright © 1954, 1958, 1962, 1964, 1965, 1987 by The Lockman Foundation. Used by permission. Scripture quotations marked ESV are taken from the ESV® Bible (The Holy Bible, English Standard Version®), copyright © 2001 by Crossway Bibles, a publishing ministry of Good News Publishers. Used by permission. All rights reserved. Scripture quotations marked NLT are taken from the Holy Bible, New Living Translation, copyright © 1996, 2004, 2015 by Tyndale House Foundation. Used by permission of Tyndale House Publishers, Inc., Carol Stream, Illinois 60188. All rights reserved. Scripture quotations marked NIV are taken from the Holy Bible, New International Version®, NIV®. Copyright © 1973, 1978, 1984, 2011 by Biblica, Inc.TM Used by permission of Zondervan. All rights reserved worldwide. www.zondervan.com. The "NIV" and "New International Version" are trademarks registered in the United States Patent and Trademark Office by Biblica, Inc.TM. Scripture quotations marked TPT are from The Passion Translation®. Copyright © 2017, 2018 by Passion & Fire Ministries, Inc. Used by permission. All rights reserved. ThePassionTranslation.com. Scripture quotations marked NLV are taken from the New Life Version, Copyright © 1969 and 2003. Used by permission of Barbour Publishing, Inc., Uhrichsville, Ohio 44683. All rights reserved. Scripture quotations marked TPT are from The Passion Translation®. Copyright © 2017, 2018 by Passion & Fire Ministries, Inc. Used by permission. All rights reserved. ThePassionTranslation.com. Scripture quotations marked NKJV are taken from the New King James Version®. Copyright © 1982 by Thomas Nelson. Used by permission. All rights reserved.

No part of this book may be reproduced, stored in a retrieval system, or transmitted by any means without written permission from the author. All rights reserved. Printed in the USA.

Rights Department, 2442 Michelle Drive, Tustin, CA 92780.

Trilogy Christian Publishing/TBN and colophon are trademarks of Trinity Broadcasting Network.

Cover design by Karis Feezell, ashes2beautyart.com

For information about special discounts for bulk purchases, please contact Trilogy Christian Publishing.

Manufactured in the United States of America

10 9 8 7 6 5 4 3 2 1

Library of Congress Cataloging-in-Publication Data is available.

ISBN: 979-8-89041-244-7

E-ISBN: 979-8-89041-245-4

DEDICATION

To the love of a lifetime, my husband, Nathan Williams. You were a tangible example of God's love in the flesh. Every soul that you encountered, you showered with the love of Christ. You were a shining example of humility and serving others. Your joy and zeal for life were contagious. I was blessed, for a season in my life, to be "one" with you. You dedicated your life to being the spiritual leader of our house, as well as showing devotion to directing other men to claim their rightful roles as the spiritual leader of their homes.

Through your death, God led me to a greater freedom. That freedom brought me to an elevated understanding of the freedom we gain through Jesus's death on the cross. I will hold on to the wisdom obtained through this journey until the day I take my very own last breath. Thank you for the example you brought to us and the inheritance you left in our lives. I love you more today than I did yesterday and a little less than I will tomorrow. I promise to never lose my joy and to continue to minister out of our heart! Until I see you again.

Love,

Your Wife

ENDORSEMENT

"The journey through loss and grief is one we will all be forced to travel. Cecily has described her journey and experience with incredible openness, honesty, and vulnerability. Her story will resonate with anyone traveling this same road. I loved her thought-provoking questions. They were brilliant and insightful and will help anyone get through this difficult journey and come out stronger. I highly recommend this book to anyone who's going through the process of loss and grief."

—Pastor Lee Armstrong

SPECIAL THANKS

Sandy Whitson (Momma)—For showing me what it looks like to carry God's presence in the middle of a storm and for standing beside me in multiple battles.

Rayelyn Whitson (my daughter)—For being a constant reminder of God's blessings in life, an example of pure joy, and a cheerleader for many. My built-in bestie and greatest gift. "Chickens are always two times the money."

Pastor Lee Armstrong—For being a Father in Faith, a safe place for guidance, and one who holds me accountable while constantly pouring out His love.

Pastor Cami Cantu—For seeing God in me above anything else and always being a source of encouragement and inspiration.

Pastor Zach Backues—For always shooting straight with me and being willing to deliver the hard messages while wrapping them in God's love.

Susan Dollery—For years of prophetically speaking God's direction over my life and being a friend.

Michelle Camp—For counsel and reigniting a fire in me for inner healing.

The Writer's Group—Together until the end, ladies!

TABLE OF CONTENTS

Chapter 1: Crystal Pain of the Departure 11

Chapter 2: Crystal Pain of the Empty Vase 19

Chapter 3: Crystal Pain of Moving Forward 27

Chapter 4: Crystal Pain of the Revolving Door 37

Chapter 5: Crystal Pain of the Spiritual War 53

Chapter 6: Crystal Pain of Recognizing the Narcissistic Spirits 65

Chapter 7: Crystal Pain of Flanking 73

Chapter 8: Crystal Pain of Re-Discovering Who You Are 85

Chapter 9: Crystal Pain of Animalistic Instinct 101

Chapter 10: A Time of Intimacy with Him 111

Chapter 11: Crystal Pain of New Birth 119

Chapter 12: Crystal Pain through the Generations 129

Bonus Chapters: A Crystal-Clear Reflection of God
within the World Today 143

Chapter 13: Crystal Pain of Being Crushed 145

Chapter 14: Crystal Pain of Repeating History 151

Chapter 15: Crystal Pain of the Beast 161

Chapter 16: Crystal Pain of Discerning the Body 169

My Journal through Grief 179

CHAPTER 1

CRYSTAL PAIN
OF THE DEPARTURE

There were six inspections during the making of *Waterford Crystal*. If any of these stages aren't perfect, the piece is then smashed and sent back into the furnace for re-melting. Have you ever felt like you made it to the sixth stage in life just to be smashed again and thrown back into the fiery furnace? That is kind of what grief feels like. Your world comes crashing down, and all the pieces of your once beautiful life's puzzle you see scattered all over, wondering how to put them back together again. If you are like me and so many others, you might feel like this is not your first trip back to the furnace.

The misconception here is that God takes things from us and then throws us in the fire for reconstruction. He will use the fire to mold us and perfect us, but He never takes what He has given and purposely causes us pain. I think that is the first thing we need to know about grief and loss. God did not put this on us!

In the winter of 2018, my husband and I had just finished building our dream home and knew the Lord told us this home would be a house of healing and restoration. During the building process, we wrote scriptures on the framework of the house and all over the foundation. We saw it as a place where people would gather, and hearts would be healed. It would be a place where people would encounter the love of the Lord, and their hearts would be touched with greater faith. Little did we know that less than a year later, we would be facing the biggest battle of our lives.

That next May, while my husband Nathan and I were attending a conference, he noticed that he was struggling with seeing the people on stage clearly. At first, we thought maybe it was the lights from the stage, but over the weekend, it gradually started to get worse. After months of doctors' visits and stays in the hospital trying to figure out what was wrong, we found out his brain was swelling. In October 2019, Nathan was diagnosed with one of the rarest forms of brain cancer. We were informed it was located in his brainstem and was inoperable and incurable.

We were not shaken! We knew we served a God of miracles and that this would be turned into a stepping-stone. My husband ran a ministry for men, and we believed he would speak on this very trial, lives would be touched, and God would get the glory! We called together the elders of our church and all our prayer warriors. We took our stance in battle and did not waver. We took communion together daily and had people across the world praying in agreement for his healing.

During the following months, we made trips daily to Dallas for radiation. My husband's health started to digress. We slowly saw him lose his ability to walk, talk, and see, and after just two months, he was sent home to hospice care, bedridden.

It is important that you know Nathan was one that walked with a servant's heart. He loved to serve and would help anyone at the drop of a hat. He was a doer and was always fixing, building, and serving others. He got more pleasure out of giving than receiving. As his wife, I was spoiled by his acts of service and was often on the receiving end of his giving gift.

Crystal Pain of the Departure

With this said, being bedridden and having to be served by his wife, children, and other family was not his idea of fun. It was almost torture for him. What you don't know about Nathan is that he was dealt a fair amount of rejection in his life, and it was during this time I knew God was showing him that there is nothing that you have to do to be worthy of extreme love. You see, Nathan showed his love by serving others, and God allowed him to see the love others had for him in those last days through the language he understood most, acts of service. There was one moment while I was bathing him one evening when he looked at me and said, "God has used this to grow our love, and it's stronger than ever. I see how much you love me." We held each other at that moment, and I cried.

Nathan and I were married later in life, and our family was a blended one. He had three children of his own, and I had one. We were both a blessing to each other and had come out of difficult times. Even with us being a blessing, we brought our own strongholds into our marriage together and had several things we had to work through. One of those strongholds for Nathan was a fear of rejection and me leaving him, as he had experienced in his past relationships. He now knew that no matter what, I would never leave him! At that very moment, the lie the enemy had spoken to him during our years of marriage was shattered, and Nathan knew the truth.

Nathan ran our 501c3, "Brothers in Christ Outdoors." It was a ministry dedicated to bringing the men of the household together and encouraging them to take their rightful roles as the spiritual leaders of the home. God showed Nathan that men would more likely open up around a campfire talking about hunting and fishing than they would in a traditional church setting. We traveled together around the U.S., and it was beautiful seeing God flow through him. One of the ways God did this was through the organization's Facebook page. Nathan often wrote devotionals on the page, and

Crystal Pain

his writings found a lot of favor with the followers.

During the last month and a half of Nathan's battle with cancer, he managed to write two devotional books. He was bedridden and completely paralyzed except for his right hand. That didn't stop him. He used that right hand to type up two books. It was his way of telling Satan, "You can take out my earthly body, but the calling to reach those for Christ will live on through these books." God has touched these books greatly, and they are divinely inspired by God's Word. However, the most beautiful thing about it was witnessing him write them.

(See Journal Entry "Inheritance of Wisdom" on page 191)

I think too often, we can judge a believer's faith based on the wrong circumstances. We say they are a man of great faith because they overcame a great obstacle and came out on top. But what qualifies as "on top"? Is it only those who are healed of the disease? Is it only those whose marriage makes it through infidelity? Is it only those who didn't lose their job?

What about those who stood in faith and gave God praise in the middle of the fiery furnace? What about those who stood giving glory to the Lord even when they were in pain? What about those, like my husband, who lay on his deathbed, paralyzed, and yet continued to raise his one functioning hand to worship music, giving honor to God? For even if the miracle didn't manifest, he knew, GOD IS GOOD! He continued to do God's work until the end.

Crystal Pain of the Departure

Hebrews 11 talks about men of bold faith. It mentions Noah, Moses, and Abraham. They were men who stood and came out of the fire unharmed! What we often fail to see is the end of that chapter. It tells us the true heroes are the ones who lost everything they possessed and endured great afflictions and were cruelly mistreated. These are the ones, it says, that should be commended for their faith. They lived in hope without receiving the fullness of what was promised.

My husband's mentor and one of our great pastors, Lee Armstrong, mentioned in one of his sermons that during a natural war, when a soldier is killed during great combat, we often award them with a purple heart. They are given a medal of honor. Should we not do the same for those soldiers of God's army that stood in faith and battled the great enemy, all while offering up praises to the one and only true God?

I know that I saw my husband battle with great faith. About a week before Nathan passed away, I was upset with the Lord. I yelled out to Him while sitting on Nathan's hospice bed placed in our living room. I screamed, "Where are you, God? This is not what your words tell us! Why are you not moving? Do you not care"! Nathan grabbed me and pulled me close to him. He said, "You can get mad, and you can be sad but don't lose your joy. Your joy is your witness, and you promise me you will not give up on God. One day, this will all make sense. Minister, out of OUR heart now." That is something that will stay with me until I take my very own last breath. Joy is a fruit of the spirit. It is not something we have to gain; we just choose to submit to the Lord, and it will manifest. We have a choice to make. We can choose to say everything in God's Word is false, we can choose to say we don't have enough faith to move mountains, or we can choose to say that some things in this earthly walk are mysteries, but God is still in it, and He is still good! Sometimes you just have to choose to trust Him. Don't give up on believing that one day we will be united with Him, and we will see the fullness of all He was doing, and it will make sense!

As mentioned, prior to my husband becoming sick, we had just built our dream home. Our house was built with a knowing

Crystal Pain of the Departure

that God told us it would be a house of restoration and healing. He showed us great gatherings of people who would come and witness God's love and presence. That is exactly what happened. In the last few days of Nathan's life, hospice told me to contact the family and let them know this would be when they needed to say their goodbyes. Within a few hours, my house was full of people, over twenty at a time. Some I barely knew, and some I knew greatly. They were all there because they loved my husband and saw God's presence in his life prior to and during these last hours. My home was filled with love, and we saw much restoration happen. One was within my husband and my own hearts as we grew together those last months, and another was just the restoration of other family members. I can only consciously speak of those that directly affected me, and for the disclosure of others, will keep it brief.

During this time, my house was filled with all of Nathan's family and friends. My parents had recently moved several states away and were not able to come very quickly. My only other near relative, I'd not been on close terms for many years. This was mainly due to my stubborn headedness. As I was watching my husband take his last struggling breaths and so desperately aching for my family to be by my side, I heard someone in the crowd around me say a phrase that echoed in my soul. They said, "A brand-new Camaro just pulled up." I knew that it was my brother. He always had Chevrolet Camaros growing up and was gifted in rebuilding cars. He had just recently bought a new one. At that point, I dropped everything that was in my hand and bolted out my front door, not stopping until I saw him get out of that car. He embraced me, and I felt the healing forgiveness he had for me, and I broke. He held me and told me he was there and would not leave me. Tears streamed down my face. That restoration will forever be something I praise the Lord for.

You see, often, God gives us a word or a vision of our future,

Crystal Pain

but He only gives us it in part. Had I known that the house God was letting Nathan and I build was going to bring forth healing and restoration in the manner it unfolded, the flesh inside me would have never built it. We just have to trust Him. I don't know that God originally intended healing and restoration to come about the way it did, but what I do know is when He gives a word, there is no force in hell that can prevent it from happening.

Waterford Crystal is made from glass being placed in a hot fiery furnace and shaped and molded into a one-of-a-kind piece. There is a skilled craftsman that etches each line on the outside into a priceless work of art. I believe that if we truly submit our lives to God, He will remove us from the fire, and as our Master Craftsman, He will take each painful etch of life's battles and create a priceless work of art. Ecclesiastes tells us, "He has made everything beautiful in its time. He has also set eternity in the human heart; yet no one can fathom what God has done from beginning to end" (Ecclesiastes 3:11, NIV).

CHAPTER 2

CRYSTAL PAIN OF THE EMPTY VASE

Shortly after the funeral, my home was filled with flowers, casseroles, family, and friends. But the thing I remember most was how it was filled with emptiness. My husband's laughter, his positivity, his wisdom, and support he poured out on everyone were GONE. The most difficult thing I remember is the emptiness in a home that once held our dreams. What did I do now? Who was I without him? How could this be my reality? A sense of disbelief was shadowing me. This couldn't be real. I was filled with questions. Yes, I even questioned God. Things didn't line up with what I thought I knew about my Father God's character. After all, He was a good Father, one who healed and showered blessings down on us, a rewarder of faith. This felt like punishment, a stripping away of blessings. How could this be MY God? The God I spent years worshipping and teaching others about His goodness? My husband and I dedicated our lives to spreading His Word, stepping out as His vessels. We wanted nothing more than to be used for His glory! He had given us a clear vision for the future, and we saw these things come to fruition. Sitting in this emptiness, I often heard my husband's words echoing in my head, "Minister out of OUR heart now." "How?" I asked. My foundation was shaken!

Crystal Pain

I heard that losing a loved one often feels like having a limb amputated. You are always aware that your arm or leg is missing, but you learn new ways to live without it. God began to show me that the recovery process after a loss is often mirrored in the process someone takes after surgery or amputation. It would require baby steps and a lot of therapy. There could be frustration and lots of falls along the way. You relearn basic skills and train your body to function in new ways to accomplish its original design. Walking may be hindered and slow, but not impossible. With the proper mindset and a determination to succeed, it can be accomplished. There was a point in this emptiness that I had to say. I WILL NOT be tethered to grief! I WILL walk again! I WILL fulfill my original design! That's what Nathan would want!

(See Journal Entry "I Will Stewart All I Gained" on page 184)

My amputation recovery would start with a liquid diet, much like how a physician would recommend directly after surgery until you can digest more food without your body rejecting it. My faith was shaken. I was nauseous and needed a gentle reminder of God's goodness and love. Although I saw myself prior to this loss as one who fed greatly on the meat of the word, I was stepping back and needed to return to a diet of milk. The pillars of my life were shaken, and it was going to take a season of refreshing my knowledge of the elementary (yet foundational) truths of God's Word. Father led me to Hebrews 5.

"In fact, though by this time you ought to be teachers, you need someone to teach you the elementary truths of God's Word all over again. You need milk, not solid food!" (Hebrews 5:12, NIV)

I believe God gave me this warning early because grief can often snap you back into a place of being hyper-focused on the cares of the world. If your journey is one where you stood on faith for healing, you more than likely found yourself growing very close to God in these times. For my husband and me, we were standing on scripture, speaking these out daily, going into prayer constantly, holding Papa God's hand 24/7, and taking communion with Him daily. We were surrounding ourselves with worship music and giving God control of our atmosphere, inviting Him to fill it with His spirit. We covered ourselves in the armor of God and fought daily alongside Him in the battle against cancer. Seeing an alternative outcome to what you were standing and believing for has a way of knocking you on your face. You're tempted to question everything you KNEW as truth and switch your focus from the ways of God's kingdom back to the ways of the world. It can look as though Satan won the battle. If you don't watch it, you can find yourself overwhelmed with the cares of the world. As the old saying goes, "Milk does a body good." BUT I was not drinking my milk!

Medical, funeral, and utility bills started rolling in; things started to pile up around the house; the responsibilities that I once shared with my spouse I was doing all alone. There was a great temptation to partner with fear, and it was easier because my thoughts became saturated with the reality of our battle's outcome not being what we were desiring and standing for. Self-Focus took over.

I personally had a hard time and got stuck in this area. I began to become very depressed and guilt-stricken. It started with recalling things I wish I wouldn't have said, as well as all the things I didn't do for Nathan that I wish I would have but now don't have the opportunity to do so. A lot of my depression was revolving around "self." I started feeling sorry for myself and the life I was being made to walk now. I would forget to depend on Jesus for my everything, or maybe I was still questioning this. I began to search for strength and hope in anything I could find. Prior to this trial, God was my go-to, my everything, the only thing I knew to find my hope and strength. But now I found myself wavering back and forth between grabbing God's hand to fill my voids and wanting to give up, questioning if it even mattered.

Crystal Pain

"But when you ask, you must believe and not doubt, because the one who doubts is like a wave of the sea, blown and tossed by the wind" (John 1:6, NIV).

My boat was all over the place. Grief can take you to a very vulnerable state. You can feel like a wounded, fearful fawn searching for the covering of its mother. Fawns are often found bedded down in areas that are exposed to great danger after becoming estranged from their mothers. This leaves them very vulnerable to the attacks of predators. So many times in my walk through grief, I found myself feeling like one of these fawns. I felt abandoned, alone, misunderstood, depressed, and full of anxiety. I found I was often not filling these voids properly with the things of God. In my mistakes, I left myself open to the attack of the enemy. Things that I had walked through in my life prior to being saved began to resurface. I was tempted to fill these voids with things I had already been delivered from after giving my life to the Lord. I often found, too, that there were people that came around that took great advantage of me, stealing from me, robbing my house of my belongings, and using me for their gain.

I hope you don't read about these attacks I went through and see familiarity. I don't want others to question how loved they are by God. Don't question the power God has entrusted to you. He draws close to the broken-hearted, and there can be a great shift that happens in this reality. There can be great growth and a huge platform available to be a witness to His glory in this journey. My husband's favorite scripture was, "Be on the alert, stand firm in the faith, act like men, be strong. All that you do must be done in love" (1 Corinthians 16:13–14, NASB). How do you flow in love when you are still questioning God's love for you? Drink your milk!

My life was like a beautiful crystal vase that once carried a bouquet of flowers. A bouquet that was filled with dreams, visions, and the perfect tribe of people to see them executed. Looking at

Crystal Pain of the Empty Vase

the empty vase now, with the bouquet gone, I was tempted to toss the vase. Or at least sit it under the counter. After all, I didn't have anything to put in it anymore. My vision and dreams were gone! The tribe I once was surrounded by had changed. Would I perish? Who am I now?

These are all questions that I had to face. The first one was WHO AM I? My life had become so engulfed with my late husband's life, intertwined as we are instructed to do when two become one in marriage. I could no longer recognize the differences between my gifts and callings and those that Nathan brought into the relationship.

The only thing I had left was the vase that carried us. That vase is Jesus. A great place to start. For it was He who held my visions and dreams. It was He who created me and deposited gifts inside me. It was He who used my life experiences to develop inside of me the knowledge and yearning to do something greater in this world. Something, deep down, told me that Jesus would do it again!

One of my husband's greatest mentors and published author, Pastor Lee Armstrong, wrote the book *The Right Questions*. I found this book to be one of the most influential books in my journey. The guidance I received through this book set me on a path that allowed me to see the things I naturally still carried. God revealed that all the answers that I was searching for were inside me. He placed them there, and they never left. I just had to ask better questions. I needed to recognize what brings me joy and even what brings me anger. Also, I needed to remember the things that make time fly for me and that by trying new things and getting planted in a community, I'd be pointed in the right direction to see what makes me, me. The things God had equipped me with would give birth to new vision.

I highly recommend this book to anyone, especially those

Crystal Pain

walking through loss. I recommend not only reading it but applying the teachings to your life. If not this book, seek out ways of rediscovering what makes you, you. In the years to come, I had to go through an extensive discovery process, but God was so faithful in it. Never give up on knowing your life has significate value. Most of the time, we are looking for something that is right in front of us the whole time.

Losing your spouse or another loved one can almost feel like you're starting over in life. Like you've been wiped clean of all your previous dreams and visions, and it's very startling. You might find yourself unable to make out what your future is supposed to look like now. If they played a major role in your life, you can even question who you are without them. It is a new beginning, a starting over, a back to the drawing board, and a clean slate that is used to hold a perfectly mapped-out plan. It's a new birth. As mentioned previously, God told me to drink my milk. What exactly is the milk of the Word? Why do I need to return to milk?

"So, abandon every form of evil, deceit, hypocrisy, feelings of jealousy, and slander. In the same way that nursing infants cry for milk, you must intensely crave the pure spiritual milk of God's Word. For this 'milk' will cause you to grow into maturity, fully nourished and strong for life especially now that you have had a taste of the goodness of the Lord Jehovah and have experienced his kindness" (1 Peter 2:1–3, TPT).

I know what I thought when I first read that. I don't feel like you were kind, God. It wasn't kind to allow my husband to die. It doesn't feel very kind walking this path I am on. It feels cruel. I had become angry and mad at God. Forgetting all the things He had graciously poured out on me over the years and how He always showed up for me in abundance. I had forgotten that death on this earth was the beginning of eternal life for my husband. One filled with the awe of the Lord's glory. I had become self-focused

Crystal Pain of the Empty Vase

and allowed bitterness, guilt, shame, anger, resentment, fear, control, and much more to cloud my vision. The milk of the word is described as repentance, faith in God, healing, and Jesus' death on the cross that allows us to walk in freedom. Unforgiveness can not only destroy you, but it can block healing. I personally was holding on to guilt, too, feeling as if I could have changed the outcome or that I wasn't a good enough wife. There are over a hundred scriptures in the Bible about bitterness and unforgiveness.

(See Journal Entry "Drink More Milk" on page 248)

You must repent of these first before healing can take place. So many times, we do not realize we are still harboring them. We may be praying for something and not see it manifest and never truly understand that the things we have erected within us to cope with pain are keeping out more than the pain. They are blocking the blessings of God. If they go unattended for too long, they can show up as illnesses within your physical body. God is often standing there with all you have asked for, but your soul is unable to receive it.

In the following chapters, I will go into depth on each one of these subjects. By using my journey as an example, I will highlight the keynotes that are referenced when describing the Milk of God's Word. I will show how the process of understanding repentance, faith in God, healing, and Jesus' death on the cross allows us to walk in freedom. I believe these are vital to anyone's walk through trauma. God never wanted us to strive through this, but I believe He understands all the obstacles that we come up against. He is patient and so gracious to pour out much wisdom on us during this journey. We just need to stay focused and yoked to Him.

"Take my yoke upon you, learn from me, for I am gentle and humble in heart, and you will find rest for your souls" (Matthew 11:29, NIV).

I hope to expose the blocks and traps that the enemy sets be-

Crystal Pain

fore us. More importantly, I hope by sharing my story, you feel empowered in your grief journey. I pray you can see a clearer path to freedom and gain the ability to recognize any hurdles that have been put in place to blur your vision or knock you off course. God will be there with open arms to hold you and walk you through. He will bring peace to those areas you struggle with. If this is too difficult to do alone, seek out a friend or pastor, or even a counselor. Remember that anything left in the dark remains under the control of darkness. It is my prayer that many things are brought out of darkness, and God shines His healing light on them. I desire more than anything for Him to once again be made real to you in all His glory.

CHAPTER 3

CRYSTAL PAIN
OF MOVING FORWARD

One of the first things I heard was that you don't ever get over grief. You just learn to move forward in it. You learn to conquer denial, anger, and depression and finally come to a place of acceptance. Many books were handed to me, mailed to me, or just showed up on my doorstep. They talked about the five stages of grief. I read these with intensity, looking for something to help me "get over" the pain. They vaguely showed me what stage I was in, but often I felt like I was in all five phases in the matter of one week. Sometimes I felt them all in one day. To be completely honest, in the initial rawness of grief, the fog caused me to lack clarity in seeing what stage I was in. Did that even matter? Was there really a timeline, process, or ladder you climbed to reach the top? Would knowing the stage help me move on to the next in hopes of getting free?

There was a point in this moving forward that it seemed I had been walking with my head down. I was so determined not to let grief define me or to get tethered to it. I was trying to live in the moment, not wanting to look to my future. I didn't know how to even picture a new life. The previous life I was forced to let go of was one I had dreamed of for years. It was a major victory and an-

Crystal Pain

swered prayer I had desired for over ten years of my life. Starting over was something I was not sure how to do. Honestly, I didn't know if I even had the strength to do it.

I realized early on, as many do after a loss, that life is short. I wanted to enjoy it before it was gone. I convinced myself that I wanted to stop wasting precious time striving for another dream, living my life in pursuit of happiness as if it was a destination I had to arrive at. I wanted to just "BE" and enjoy what was right in front of me. I wanted to let things happen naturally and stop trying to manipulate the situation to bring about a vision.

I was in a counseling session during the first months of my journey with Pastor Zach Backues. Pastor Zach is someone that has walked me through many stages of life. He knows that with me, when I come to him, I am seeking to be held accountable and for someone to shoot straight with me. I admire him with much esteem because he has a way of holding me accountable and not sugarcoating anything while wrapping his delivery with an obvious love of God. In this session, he mentioned that my husband's death would be used to bring me freedom. It would be like a fresh chance to change all the negative things I was harboring in relation to our marriage. He informed me that he felt I was dealing with guilt and needed to forgive myself. Guilt was another stage I experienced in grief. One of those things I carried was the guilt of constantly pushing my husband and me to conquer the next step. We often skipped family vacations to work on ministry instead. There was always one more thing we needed to get accomplished before we could rest. I carried a lie inside me that we had to earn our rest. I placed a lot of pressure on my husband too.

So, here I was, starting over. Knowing I was hearing God in many ways. He was giving me great wisdom, and I knew it was Him. I knew I had to stop striving and know that my gifts are things that come naturally to me. I had to just "BE" who He created me

Crystal Pain of Moving Forward

to be. I was to stop thinking that I had to earn my rest and that joy was not a destination that I had to arrive at. At that moment, I saw a new way of operating out of grace, and I was determined to lay down the perfectionistic mindset that had gripped me for years. I wanted to stop thinking that there was a formula to God's ways that I had to walk in, or else I failed. Was this a taste of the freedom my pastor was referring to?

I finally saw the direction for my next step. But like so many times in my life, I jumped forward, thinking I got this! It was like I had a therapy session with God and left the office waving to Him on my way out, saying, "I got it. If I need you, I'll make another appointment; thanks for the directions." I forgot that living a Spirit-filled life is just that. It's a constant walk with His presence. You don't just wake up and get the blueprints to life and call on the developer once you make a mistake. He must be involved in every placement of each board. One inch off, and it could cause the entire new build to come crumbling down. He wants to walk hand in hand with us. He wants this! It's not a burden on Him; it's not an obligation of His. It's His desire. He is omnipresent and with us at all times, in all places. It's the desire of His heart. He made us create and build with Him.

A lot of times, as a widow, you can come across the lie that you need to learn to be independent again. You start believing that fending for yourself is part of the process. But there is a reason that so many times throughout the Bible, God instructs His people to care for the widows and the fatherless. Community and asking for help are direct reflections of our relationship with God. He is our husband and our provider. He is our help in times of trouble. He is our comfort and our strength. He flows through His people and His church, and it is in that that the world around us experiences a tangible example of what His heart looks like in the flesh. We can't sit back and expect the help to just show up, but it does require something of us. It requires our humility, our dying to our flesh,

Crystal Pain

and our ability to ASK for assistance. It requires us to reach out and partner with Him. It requires us to partner with His church and His bride. He tells us, "Ask and it will be given to you; seek, and you shall find; knock, and it will be opened unto you" (Matthew 7:7, ESV). That help comes to us in the form of His people. Just as we are to be that very help to others.

Years ago, I was blessed to have beautiful mentors while training in leading mission teams. One of them gave me a piece of advice that I still hear in my heart today. She said, "You can go fast and go alone, or you can go far and go together." I believe God desires to take us farther than we can ever imagine. It's those times when you reach your breaking point and are at a point of exhaustion that you need to stop and ask, "Have I been going at this alone, and am I humble enough to ask for help?"

Let's break that phrase down by revisiting the first part. "You can go fast and go alone." It's a temptation, isn't it? We want to go fast. We want to get through the process quickly, finish the race, and receive the benefits of our labor. We want to be rewarded, to bask in the glory of our triumph. We want to stand on the podium and be showered with applause for our accomplishments. How quickly pride can attach itself to a person in great sorrow. It's especially easy for the enemy to see the unhealed wounds and want to pounce. What better way to take out a child of God than to get them when they are already wounded? He doesn't sit back and give you a break while you're healing. This is another reason you need community. You need a tribe, or maybe a more fitting term for this analogy would be PRIDE. Just like lions live in a group called pride. Our pride comes from the KING of KINGS. Our pride is composed of fellow believers and includes the lion of Judah.

(See Journal Entry "Massaging Out Pride" on page 246)

Isn't it just like the enemy to take the progress and wisdom

Crystal Pain of Moving Forward

that we gain from God and bring in a counterfeit? He comes in and distorts the truths oh so slightly. He knows that if he can get us to drink just a small amount of the contaminated substance, the entire meal can make us sick. His goal is to bring death to any life God is depositing in us. I can, of course, only speak on my journey and know that it is not an all-encompassing dialogue for everyone's grief journey. However, in hopes of sharing my errors and deceptions, I hope it opens the eyes of those who are wounded to see the slight schemes and ways of the enemy. My hope is to shed light on the importance of being sober-minded and alert and remaining surrounded by others who see clearly while you are healing. Be open to their corrections and hear their hearts. Not everyone will understand your emotions or pains. I do believe, however, that there are many who see the enemy and have been placed in the family of believers to be these watchmen for others. They are there to remind us of our authority and, most importantly, the power that flows in submitting to God's healing waters of love that rescue us out of all darkness.

The word tells us that where there is no clear prophetic vision, people quickly wander astray (Proverbs 29:18, TPT). The word "prophetic" means: accurately describing or predicting what will happen in the future (Oxford Language Dictionary). I used to run a women's clothing store, and we would go to the fall market in the heat of July. I would invest thousands of dollars in what the vendors were telling me the trends would be for the upcoming season. I made sure I invested my money with companies that I knew had a big impact on the industry and, time and time over, had proven to be successful in predicting these trends. I wasn't going to take a chance on just any vendor. These vendors had withstood the tests of time and earned influence in the market across the board. They were well-known by the masses. They were vendors you might even know to this day, brands like Steve Madden, Betsey Johnson, and RayBan. I knew that if I was going to place the success of my business in the hands of another, I wanted it to be someone that I trusted. Someone that wasn't still learning the market and was still wobbly on their feet. There were many times when I first opened my store that I bought things out of pure emotion and didn't seek counsel. I moved purely on my fleshly instinct. Those items sat in my store and didn't sell. It was a waste of money. After time, I was able to know my market and what my clientele preferred and could buy with ease, but not when I first started learning.

Your life is precious to the Lord. It is one He wants to invest in. He also wants to make sure that His vision of your future lies in the hands of someone that is not wobbly on their feet. When He entrusts this vision to you, He wants to ensure that the first source of advice you reach for comes from someone you trust and has proven time and time again to show success. That person is Jesus. He wants to be the person you look to first for guidance. Yes, the confirmation of what He is showing you can come from others in the industry, but His instruction should be the foundation of that advice. It's important not to rush the process and get frustrated in the waiting or frustrated in the healing. If we move out of God's timing, operate out of pure emotion, or try and create our own step-by-step guide to get through quicker, we can open ourselves up to conceiving a counterfeit. Anything that is artificially created will have to be artificially sustained or might end up sitting there on the shelf and collecting dust.

I said earlier in this chapter that I had gotten to a place in my moving forward where I was walking with my head down. I wanted to just live in the moment. I wanted to cherish what was right in front of me and had stopped looking for a destination to arrive at to find joy. These are not necessarily bad things. They are a beautiful way of living if done correctly, as explained above. However, I want to shine a light on how the enemy came in and distorted these truths along my journey.

Crystal Pain of Moving Forward

So, here I was, walking the healing journey, hearing God's wisdom, and seeing Him reveal Himself. I was proud of my progress. I was determined to not be stuck in this hell called widowhood. What's my new vision, God? I had nothing to lose. The loss of my husband and partner in these ministries quickly was followed by a pruning of all things of that life. I turned over the 501c3 to a fellow pastor and my husband's mentor, closed the store that I used in the marketplace to reach our community for Christ, and I even sold some of the investment properties that we had seen God use to prosper us financially which gave us the ability to pour into the community in a monetary form. I felt stripped of anything that I found identity in. I found myself looking at not only my life but the world around me and seeing nothing that looked familiar. My heart was crying out for something, anything that was familiar.

This was all happening in the middle of the COVID-19 pandemic. The echo around the world was "Finding our New Normal." Now this was already a common phrase for anyone who was walking through widowhood, only now the entire world was walking through this. We all were confined to our homes and away from the community. We were unable to avoid anything within ourselves or our family that rubbed us wrong. We couldn't run from it. There was no escape. Any fear you had, there was no distraction away from it to run to. At this time, fear was covering the world like a big black blanket. Whatever the normal vise you used to escape was closed, canceled, or shut down. Schools, churches, businesses, stores, gyms, airports, bars, everything was shut down.

I realize many people utilized this time for their benefit. They may have worked on projects around their home, spent much-needed time as a family, studied and got closer to God, or started working out more in the downtime. However, on the opposite side of that, many grew antsy, got irritated with their families, vegged out, and indulged in alcohol. Triggers and negativity were highlighted and on big display. If you had a slight issue before, the quarantine

Crystal Pain

pressure put a magnifying glass to it.

One thing I noticed being birthed out of this time was a real season of SELF. After quarantine ended and things started to go back to a fairly normal way, a wave of self-improvement, self-healing, self-growth, and becoming the best version of yourself era started. It was like the mindset I developed after losing my husband. There was an awareness that life is short, and we need to enjoy it while it lasts. This just "Be" and "You do You" idealism was everywhere you turned. It was saturating our social platforms and invading mainstream media. Included in this was the move of exposing the narcissist. Everywhere you turned, someone was exposing narcissistic abuse. They either claimed to be a victim of narcissistic abuse or a self-aware narcissist that was shedding light on the subject. It only makes sense that the enemy deposited eggs of self-focus in the isolation stage of this pandemic. What better breeding ground for his maggots of pride to hatch?

(See Journal Entry "Early Detection of Spiritual Warfare Birthed in Pride" on page 203)

What I believe God could have used as a time of us facing those things inside us that needed submitting to Him for healing and truth to be spoken over, a period of transforming our triggers, wounds, fears, and irritants into beautiful pearls of wisdom and growth, the enemy came into and mixed pride into the batter. He contaminated this beautiful recipe and turned it into something rotten. He found ways of masquerading the traditions of darkness as forms of light. You saw an influx of New Age trends, psychic and tarot card readings, energy and reiki healings, etc. These were practices that held a look of promise but possessed a slight distortion that leaned you ever so slightly away from the truth. They held something that said, I, in myself, can produce the change I want. It was something that removed God from the equation and replaced it with idolization and self-power. The sad thing is many of us fell for the counterfeit. We sat down at the table and dined with the entire army of lies that were prepared, myself included.

"When your soul is full, you turn down even the sweetest honey. But when your soul is starving, every bitter thing becomes sweet." (Proverbs 27:7, TPT)

The separation from my pride, the kind of pride that's made up of lions and lionesses of God's kingdom, a community of believers who protect each other, hold each other accountable, and help feed you the truth of the word, allowed me to step into this counterfeit pride. The one that is a doorway to destruction and wickedness. I didn't take the necessary time to allow God to heal my wounds, reveal those triggers, and use the crushing pain to bring forth the new wine he originally wanted to pour out of me. In that broken state, my rush to move forward quickly and the unsubmitted bitterness in my heart quickly got twisted. I stepped into another battle, one that almost took me out. I found myself on this battlefield fighting the legions attached to the Ring Master of Pride.

(See Journal Entry "Lead Poisoning" on page 285)

CHAPTER 4

CRYSTAL PAIN OF THE REVOLVING DOOR

My husband and I married each other later in life. Before I met him, I walked through a lot. Although I was raised in a beautiful Christian home and knew God at an early stage, I went through a real rebellious season in my adolescent and young adult years. God had gifted me with certain gifts of the spirit that my parents weren't taught about in the churches they attended. I would often see angelic beings in my room as a child. As I got older, I believe that Satan tried to stop me from using this ability by demonically attacking me. I was often choked by demons and even thrown out of my bed at one time. During one of these incidents, I hit a table in my room and sliced my eye open. My mom and dad rushed into my room, and while Mom was trying to hold me, she fainted at the sight of the blood. After that, I was unable to sleep at night. Up until the age of eight to ten years old, I would often run into my parents' bedroom in fear, asking to sleep with them. As I got older, I just wanted to be normal and live a normal life. I wanted to be like all my other friends. I didn't like being different and knew I couldn't share any of this with anyone. I rebelled against God, felt sorry for myself for being so different, and did anything in my power to drown out that I wasn't like the rest of them. My parents

Crystal Pain

thought I must be special, but I did not want that! I wanted to be like everyone else!

I rebelliously lived years in sin. I partied wildly, did drugs, was sexually active, and opened myself up to the lusts of the world. I was easily led astray. I had great Christian friends in high school, but by the time I was in college, I was finding myself in a deep depression. I was using drugs and alcohol more and more to kill the struggle. There was a pull to live for God and use these gifts for Him or succumb to the hate in my heart I had because I was different. There was a point I fully gave over to a life of sin. I had not fully understood grace and the loving mercy of God. Religion was all I knew at this time in my life. Religious teachings told me it was either perfection or failure. I couldn't be perfect, but it was easy for me to party.

This pull to share God's love never left me, even in my sinful ways. I would find myself doing lines of coke with atheists at parties and trying to share the word with them and prove God was real. One night I had several people over to my apartment, doing drugs at 5 a.m., and I remember getting the Bible out, trying to teach one of them about God. I share all this to make the point regarding a long push and pull that I struggled with in my life regarding submitting to God when things seemed too hard in the walk He assigned to me.

Initially, after I lost my husband, I saw God in every step. I arrived at a place where I felt like God and I (together) conquered the battle. Storm number two rolled around within a month. When I was thrown back in the fire with the pandemic and isolated away from my community, the enemy got me alone, and my thoughts distorted.

Shortly after that, I was again crying out. Looking back at my life searching for familiarity. Through people that came into my life, I was reintroduced to things that were familiar to me. Not from my life with my husband, but from a previous life. I was once again served temptation like a sinful delicacy. I was hearing the familiar thoughts, *wouldn't it be nice to just be normal?* There was that familiarity to stop striving to be perfect. There was that familiar voice saying, "Stop fighting the battles and just live life." I felt the craving to just live for self-gratification in return. I thought it would not hurt you to just partake in a little bit of the worldly lusts. As long as you are a good person and kind to others, you can do whatever, and God will still love you. I told myself, *No one is perfect. Stop beating yourself up and thinking you must do everything perfectly to gain God's blessings. Wouldn't it be nice to just fit in and be normal again?*

Of course, these were twisted lies. After learning God was a God of grace, and breaking free from the burden of religion, my husband and I had lived a life sold out to Him. After experiencing the overpowering love God had for me, nothing else satisfied me like being in His presence. It was funny how I quickly forgot how I hungered for God, and the things I "gave up" (according to the world) were not a struggle for me at all. They fell off easily because they didn't hold any value once compared to the lifestyle of living with God's joy. Living with God and being used by Him was the only time I truly felt I was being authentic. At this time, however, I was not living this way.

I found myself in this struggle. I had a choice to make. I knew there was a call on my life. I knew that God could turn the pains I recently walked through into testimony. I even started drafting this very book just two months after losing Nathan. Was I going to accept this, or was I going to rebel against the assignment God was revealing? Was I going to choose to offer my life as a living sacrifice to God, or was I going to live to satisfy the idols of my flesh?

It was during this time that a beautiful man walked into my life. He was full of life-giving energy, and my spirits lifted every

Crystal Pain

time I was in his presence. He made me laugh until my cheeks hurt. He had a way of making me feel special for just breathing. He simplified life and took me on a journey of just living in the moment. It was like tasting the little things in life for the first time all over again. I thought, *This must be what resting looks and feels like. This must be what understanding life as a gift looks like, lived out. This is just "being." Life is here for us to enjoy, and it can be taken from us in a heartbeat; just drink it in.*

The first six months of this relationship felt like a dream, like a second chance at life. When the pandemic first hit, I found myself isolated and all alone, but now I had someone. The ease of walking through the pandemic with him was unexplainable. I didn't even have a care in the world. I was even able to open up to him about how I would sense things in the spirit and sometimes see into the spirit realm. He accepted these things and even informed me that he, too, had seen things before.

Shortly after we started dating, I was sharing with him about a man dressed in total black that walked down my hall and into my living room. I was telling him how I chased after him, and this was a spirit I had never seen before. He gave me a description of him and asked if that was what he looked like. I couldn't believe how accurately he described him. He informed me that he had seen that same man in his house before and that he calls him the pilgrim. At that point, I really thought I had met someone who understood me on a level like never before.

We would always talk about how deep our connection was and that it was on a spiritual level. He'd say things like I can feel what you are feeling. He'd praise me, calling me a healer. One time we were outside my house, and I saw two giant beings standing beside us. They were about twelve feet tall. I figured he could see on my face that something was different. I told him I saw two angels. But something didn't make total sense. Any other time I saw angelic

Crystal Pain of the Revolving Door

presences, they would appear as beaming light. These particular beings were black. I let it go and didn't feel a need to analyze anything. I wasn't an expert in everything. I was just so excited about being able to share anything with him.

He was kind, encouraging, and quick to share how much he loved me. He was even patient when I wasn't quite ready to reciprocate those same words back to him. I opened up early about my fears and trials in life. I told him all my areas of weakness. I even expressed how I didn't want to strive to be in ministry anymore because I just wanted to live life. He would comfort me, saying he would support me in any decision I made. We had slightly different beliefs on several things. Topics around politics and other controversial subjects didn't exactly line up. They were close enough, though. I found myself open-minded to try to hear different viewpoints and expand mine for the first time. I was starting to lay down what I thought might have been too rigid of a way of believing and softened up to receive a more balanced view. I was willing to adopt another way of seeing things. I really liked living with him and the free spirit he was. I loved his childlike love of life and living in the moment. I did not want to let this go and was willing to do anything to hold on to it. He would say things like, "You do you, boo," and "Just be a good person, and everything will fall into place."

You see, here is where the enemy got me. If Satan can find you in a state of confusion, he can easily impart lies. If he finds you already partnering with rebellion, he can ultimately establish a platform to introduce sin back in your life. I was already confused about why I was being forced to walk this life, as well as not really joyful about having to. I also was rebellious in my nature at this point. I was dabbling in the lusts of the world and walking a lukewarm lifestyle. It was the want to just be normal and not need to walk the straight and narrow, but still wanting God's blessings for myself. My focus was on me. I was focused on what the world had to offer me, and I walked away from truly being selfless in the pursuit of building God's church. I wasn't living to serve God, but I had twisted the truth into how God could serve my life.

"Be alert and of sober mind. Your enemy the devil prowls around like a roaring lion looking for someone to devour" (1 Peter 5:8, NIV).

The enemy is looking for someone to devour. He often uses disguises, twists the truths, and distorts our viewpoints. If we are not sober-minded (guarding our thoughts, casting down our imaginations, and staying fixed on the truth of God's Word), then we open ourselves up as a target. I was not doing this. In my pain, I allowed both confusion and rebellion to enter my thoughts. I wasn't staying in God's Word or surrounding myself with my church family. I might as well have run through a bull pin dressed in a red suit. I was a clear target. I knew that the man I was now spending most of my time with wasn't going to question any of my views. He would accept me as I was, no matter what that viewpoint happened to be. I liked that about him.

I'm not blaming him for this because I don't even think he saw an error in anything I might have picked up. We are not all called to walk the same path in life. We all don't carry with us the same convictions at the same time in our lives. We all travel on different roads that, if submitted to God, can lead us to specific callings. These roads come with different traumas and wounds that can affect us. I didn't think the path he was on was for me to judge. I do, however, think it's our responsibility as believers to surround ourselves with individuals and partner with people that can pour into the call on your life. We also should keep our eyes open to those things that we start tolerating and accepting that don't line up with God's direction in our own life. As for me, I knew there was more to this life than how I was living at that time. I had personally experienced it before in my life. But I turned from allowing myself to hear it, receive it, or want it. In doing this, I became very double-minded. I was struggling with knowing how I was supposed to be living and desiring to walk a separate way. I was also closed off from boldly discussing this struggle inside me with anyone. I let my fear of being judged and alone outweigh the fear of God.

As time went on, I felt that pull again from God. The gifting inside me stirring. I started to recognize more and more that some of the beliefs I started to hold were not aligning with what I previously knew as truth. One example is I started having panic attacks. I lived in Oklahoma at this time, and medical marijuana was legalized. This man I was seeing had his medical card, and I would often use his marijuana. It seemed to calm me down and allow me to experience a euphoria I had not felt in a long time. After a while, I obtained my own medical marijuana card and started smoking weed regularly to calm my nerves. This quickly became a source I turned to for comfort.

I also started working out at a gym as a source of ridding myself of anxiety, which gave birth to an unhealthy habit centered around pride rather than health. A slippery slope for many, but one God began to show me was becoming more of an addiction than a hobby. In this, I became way too obsessed with my looks. I started dressing in a more seductive manner which was the opposite of what I had before. I justified it because my boyfriend often commented on how much he liked my style. I had now placed two things in my life as sources of ridding anxiety. Even though I often heard the scripture in my heart screaming, "Cast your cares on the Lord, and He will sustain you; He will never let the righteous be shaken." I chose to ignore it. I erected these two things as idols in my life, and they were a gateway for me to accept many other things.

(See Journal Entry "Motivated by Lies" on page 272)

As time went on, I started to question my boyfriend on so many

Crystal Pain

different levels. In my head, I started to nitpick everything he did. If it didn't line completely up with what I felt a perfect Christian should be doing, it started to irritate me. I never openly voiced what I was thinking but would throw out scriptures hoping that he would see his thoughts and actions were contradictory to what God instructed us to be. At the same time, I was conscious of the fact that I wasn't living the proper way either or carrying thoughts in my heart like I was trained to. Instead of admitting this, I started projecting this guilt on him. It was as if I justified any of my wrongs by thinking if I was able to guide someone else to a better path, I was still a good person. Part of me wanted him to develop into the person I was feeling God pulling me to be, and then I could follow in his footsteps. I thought if I could get him to lead, then I wouldn't have to be alone on my own journey.

Intertwined in this, I was still dealing with wounds of loss and seeing the two different lives I lived. From my marriage, I knew that when two people enter a relationship, you often both bring strongholds into it. Those strongholds are often developed from the ways of processing things in your thoughts and actions that stem from wounds and hurts of your past. They can take time to adjust to, but we need to be there to help each other through them. If we really care for one another, we can heal together. I fell short here by not trying to talk about them when they first showed themselves. I wondered if there were things about my behavior he, too, shoved under the rug. I'm sure he felt this unacceptance I had placed on him. If there were any unhealed wounds inside him, this unacceptance could also trigger his unsubmitted trauma responses too.

I saw in him things that were similar to the needs I often dealt with. It was a need for admiration and praise for accomplishments. This stemmed from our love languages being similar, words of affirmation. I noticed sometimes he would compliment me but follow it up with a question about what I liked about him. I would get so frustrated if he did this because I thought he was just flattering me to get something in return. I pointed it out a lot when he did this. He'd laugh and say he wasn't and that he loved me is why he always told me things. I wondered if he thought I wasn't good enough because I didn't compliment him like he did me. I started to feel condemned, thinking I was failing in this area. I wanted to fulfill every desire he had. I also placed the responsibility on him to fulfill mine. From that point on, this became a regular thing I tried to maintain for him. I was doing it because I didn't want to lose him, not because it always came naturally to me. He often mentioned things he was proud of doing at work or with his kids. Even if it seemed menial in my mind, I tried to make sure I complimented him to reinforce that need. I started unknowingly carrying a responsibility to meet his needs for him.

In my mind, I continued to destroy the way he operated. I thought it was all him, unaware of the true root of what was causing these irritations in my soul. He would often say things like, "I love how you look at me" or "I love how you make me feel." Eventually, I started to question these comments too. I felt that love shouldn't be about how someone makes you feel, but it's deeper than that. It's not about what you get from someone. I wanted to be loved on the deepest level, not for my performance. I was starting to believe that it was only in my performance that he loved me, and the battle against needing to be perfect was screaming inside me. I had experienced *Agape* love before, and my heart was hungry for that void to be filled. I wanted to encounter the purity of God's love that compares to no other form.

The struggle inside me was me thinking that if I totally submitted to God and let God develop me into who He desired me to be, I would risk losing my boyfriend in that process. I eventually saw that if I was weak in an area, and my boyfriend was weak in a similar area, him being weak was a direct target against the person God wanted me to be. I thought it was his fault, not mine. What I didn't realize was what I was truly battling was not him. It was the rebellious nature inside me. I had become so self-focused I started to live to feed my flesh. I wanted compliments, I desired flattery, I wanted to feel like I was someone's main desire. I believe he desired these things from me as well.

You see, in a relationship, God should always be the center of that relationship. He should be your main source. The things you need in your soul need to first be met and filled with Him. You have to truly know who you are in God and how greatly He loves and desires you. When you know that God first loves you, then you should place seeking Him, living to serve Him, and allowing Him to flow through you to touch others at the core. In this, God often blesses you. You feel God's power engulfing each other in your every move and start to develop into that authentic image of Christ. You then walk in purity that overflows out of your relationship with God into your relationship with each other. Any other counterfeit to this type of Agape love will never sustain your relationship. It will only remove God as the source and replace Him with an idol. That idol becomes each other and what you can gain from one another. This ultimately drains a person.

I started to see that our relationship was more about serving each other first, as well as what we could get out of each other. We just put God in the mix. It wasn't us serving God and His kingdom first, with us abundantly experiencing the overflow. Somehow, I felt that SELF unconsciously had become an idol. It was about what we could gain. Whatever it was (power, social status, material things, or our dreams), they seemed to be our focus. I started to become very uncomfortable with my behavior. As mentioned, I chose to destroy him in my mind; verses see that I, too, was actively in partnership with it. I, too, was playing a role by allowing it. I was not taking responsibility for my own actions. This gave way to a full reign of confusion.

Crystal Pain of the Revolving Door

There started to be a paranormal activity in my home. I saw figures in my room, lights flickering, electronics going off simultaneously, and my dogs growling at the figures I saw. It was like my childhood. I remember grabbing my Bible and anointing oil and praying over every door in my house, commanding anything that wasn't of God to leave my house. But God only gives us authority to the measure that we have submitted to Him. I was not completely submitted to Him.

After this, my boyfriend and I were arguing more, and sometimes things in everyday conversations didn't even make sense to me. It was almost like I didn't recognize the logic or couldn't follow the pattern of thought. I would even try to say things, and he wouldn't hear them like I thought I was saying them. In my mind, it was like a cloud of total confusion between us.

By this time, we had started going to church. Stepping back into this atmosphere ignited something inside me that I knew was missing. I felt that hunger for the purity of God returning. I started reading and studying my Bible again and praying regularly. Being surrounded by corporate worship with Spirit-filled believers made me realize I was starving for someone to talk to about the Lord. I wanted to discuss how He was speaking to me. I felt that desire for the fellowship of the church and wanted to apply God's principles back into my life. An overwhelming yearning for the things I had walked away from was presenting itself. There was that push and pull inside of me again. I could feel it.

My boyfriend started reading the Bible, too. He would share briefly what he was reading. This excited me, and I so hungered to discuss this. We'd mention doing a study together, and I once bought a book for us to read. This never came to fruition, though. We could never get anything off the ground together. At one point, I told him that there were things I asked the Lord to remove from my life. I informed him that God had done this for me, and there

Crystal Pain

was no desire for it anymore. He thought that this was something we should have discussed together. I thought he was trying to keep me in sin. This discussion ended with us hanging up the phone on each other. There was a lot of tension and unresolved anger behind it. However, I tried to reflect on the situation from his viewpoint. I agree that there needs to be a discussion between partners. It can eliminate confusion. I pondered how it could have appeared strange to see your partner's behavior change abruptly and without explanation. I was able to see how it could automatically make the other feel they did something wrong. But at that moment, I only saw it as a relationship between God and me. I was then clearly aware that I didn't put us on the same level spiritually.

In the lifestyle I was presenting to him, I never clearly displayed myself as someone that wanted these things. Mainly because I never felt I could openly discuss them. I often felt like when I did try and speak about them, it was coming out like a foreign language. I would battle with trying to find the foundation to build the conversation. Especially since, previously, I'd never spoken about them in great depth. Those facts did not overshadow the urging of the Holy Spirit I was encountering, though.

I know he sensed there were two different people I was starting to portray. I knew his background wasn't like mine, and I didn't even know where to begin to give a comprehensive explanation of everything I desired back in my life. I just assumed his lack of inquiring proved he didn't desire that lifestyle. He seemed content in life; this was something that drew me to him, to begin with. He was confident in himself and at peace with his life. I figured he would never understand. Nonetheless, I wanted to step back into a lifestyle that I had previously experienced and was not willing to put my growth on hold. In fear of him rejecting it, I wasn't willing to explain anything unless he presented the hunger for it to me first.

Crystal Pain of the Revolving Door

I began to see him as the culprit of all my backsliding. I unconsciously placed all the blame on him. Of course, now I am aware of there being an actual spiritual war going on around me. At that time, I only saw a person as a hindrance. We would have an argument and end up with us hanging up the phone on each other. Then the next day, it was like it never happened. We'd never discuss it again. I inquired about the "why" to us not discussing the issue at hand in-depth, and he would say why to walk in anger. I wanted him to see the deeper root of our disconnect, but only if he truly wanted it. I would always say, I never want to change you. But deep down, I had wanted to change myself. I wanted him to want this, too. I stepped back and tried to make sure that this was a path God had us both on.

No matter how hard we tried to work things out, they eventually seemed to end up in us breaking up. As I said, I believe he had always been living a life that he was completely comfortable in. I was still very double-minded. I started looking for him to see that the way I was living didn't match how I used to be and for him to correct me. Even though he had never experienced that girl before. Inside, I felt the blame was always placed on me. If I had a problem with anything, it was rebutted with, "You don't think I'm good enough for you," "You won't teach me this or that," "How could you treat me like this," or "You're crazy and need help." I was able to see his point and felt shame for how this came across. I carried that weight. I started to believe that maybe it was me.

Still neglecting the truth regarding the push and pull of my flesh fighting surrendering fully to the Holy Spirit, I directed those beliefs elsewhere. I thought, maybe this is just my grief, and I need counseling. I didn't want to think I was better than anyone for starting to desire different things. I knew that God's Word says that you just have to believe in Him, and you are saved. As long as we both believed that we were destined for heaven. So, I read many books on trauma, got counseling, and tried to heal myself. I

Crystal Pain

realized now that I was presenting one person but struggling with the person I knew I was in Christ. I was not being true to the me that was sold out to Christ. I definitely was not consistent in displaying this person to my boyfriend, either. By this time, I was in love with this man. I was now fighting this awareness and the fact that he had such an unexplainable pull over me. Even in the arguing, I couldn't walk away. I loved him, so I stayed and tried to shove everything down. But I was growing more confused as the days went on.

One night as I was leaving the gym, I saw a homeless couple sleeping in the dead of winter on the sidewalk. I cried as I reflected back on how in my previous life, I wouldn't have walked by them without stopping to offer help. I couldn't sleep that night, thinking about how they were suffering as I was sleeping in a warm bed. I started to see that living a life just for pure enjoyment reasons wasn't enough. I recognized that there was real selfishness that I had started to partner with. I knew at that moment something had to change. I shared my concerns with my boyfriend, and he said I had a big heart but couldn't let it get to me. I felt the urgency to pour out love on the hurting and hungered to know others shared this overwhelming feeling.

Months later, I attended a women's seminar where my friend, Cami Cantu, was ministering. She and her husband pastor Faith Center Church out of Sulfur, Oklahoma. She's a powerful woman of God who operates in a huge gift of encouragement, the ability to call out the gifts in others, and a breaker anointing. She spoke over me that day, saying that I was a prophetess of God and that He would "Be It Unto Me." I remember sliding down in my chair, terrified. I knew I had not been walking this life in totality and was not yet completely surrendered to God. After she finished ministering, she called all who felt bound by something to the front. Cami laid hands on me and began to prophesy and pray over me who God said I was. I couldn't stand up under the powerful presence

Crystal Pain of the Revolving Door

of God's love that was pouring out on me, and I fell to the floor weeping. The weeping turned to deep moaning as I fell, things breaking free from deep within my gut. I was feeling the love of the Father washing over me. There was so much both broken off of me at that moment as well as just encountering the true Spirit of God. Cami, finally, after some time, came back over to me while I was in a pool of tears on the floor, and she said, "Get up in faith, Cecily, and prophesy over these other women"!

Something ignited in me that day. Something finally clicked inside me, and I was able to fully see that there was something more I was created for. I knew that it would look different, but that desire was deposited back inside me, and that day it took root. I was shaky but got up and, in faith, started to prophesy and pray over others. Cami had just taught us about the Father "Being it Unto Us." She spoke about if God has given us an assignment in life, then it is He who equips and flows through us. We are just to be submitted and obedient. The shift was redirected off me, back to being a vessel for God to touch others. What I was feeling was a realignment of my selfish focus back to the true heart of the Father. It was the one that was focused on His kingdom. When you experience and embrace the magnitude of God's love for you, the great commission shifts from feeling like an assignment you are obligated to fulfill to an extension of a lifestyle you have been blessed to share in.

CHAPTER 5

CRYSTAL PAIN OF THE SPIRITUAL WAR

I thought that coming back to God would be easy. What I didn't know was the degree to which my backsliding had opened me up to spiritual warfare. These spirits were not going to let me go that easily. They saw me rebelling and partnering with the kingdom of this world. Satan was not about to lose the ground he thought he had gained in my life. He would use anything and anyone to try and make this impossible for me. The struggle was extremely hard. Due to the unexplainable pull that I had toward my boyfriend, I chose to just go completely no contact. I walked away after our last argument for the final time. It was so hard because a part of me wanted to try again and explain why to him. I didn't want to be that person, but I knew if I spoke to him, the outcome would be just like every other time. I would go right back into the relationship. I was smart enough to see that whether it was me and my trauma or if it was his unhealed wounds, we together were not a good combination. I had enough evidence in both my spirit and physical experiences that I knew I needed to get out of that relationship. I can only speak with confidence about my errors in the relation-ship. Without going into details, I did encounter things within his actions that I did not have to put up with anymore. I was no longer going to allow myself to be controlled out of fear of a person or any spirits in operation between us. That included the fear of being alone and walking a path God called me to by myself. Nothing was going to stop me from being obedient to God anymore. I also knew I was weak when it came to this man; there was a soul tie that developed that was strong. Until I knew God had broken that tie, I blocked his number from my phone and all his social media platforms.

He came to my home after three weeks of no contact, knocking on all my doors. Before he left, he put a note on my car. I remember being so afraid that I hid in my closet the entire time. My body was trembling, and I was crying. Something made me call the sheriff's department and my neighbor, who was a reserve police officer. My neighbor came over seconds after he finally left and advised me to put up cameras and get a gun. He told me that if I was shaking in the manner I was, that was my intuition that I didn't need to ignore. He felt this would not be his last time to try and contact me, and it wasn't. At this point, I didn't truly understand why I was shaking so badly, but I was in terror. I remembered that there were other times during the relationship I'd experienced this too. Whether it was during anger outbursts or times I was trying to get him to leave my house after an argument. This was a familiar feeling.

I noticed in all the attempts to contact me, be it leaving messages on my car or the numerous amount I found on my phone under blocked messages, he never once had a concern for me or asked if I was okay. These messages only displayed focus on himself. His focus seemed to be on what he looked like to others, how he was feeling, how I was disrespecting him, and what he felt he deserved. I realize now that I wanted him to be someone he wasn't. I was able to self-reflect and often destroyed myself in the process. After these statements, I questioned my motives. Had I been guilty of the same selfish focus that I saw in him?

Crystal Pain of the Spiritual War

Was I more concerned about what my church family was thinking of me, how they would judge my walk, and what I wasn't getting from him? I walked away because I saw him as detrimental to my walk with the Lord. I saw him as a hindrance that was pulling me down. I was certain a part of him knew this. He expressed that I thought I was chosen and he wasn't a good enough Christian. But I would hate myself if I thought I was better than anyone. God calls us to help others and share His love with all. Mentally this was torturing me.

The entire time I battled between condemning myself for being a horrible person and feeling I was picking up on something I needed to run far away from. I was beating myself up for choosing to live a certain lifestyle, not staying true to my identity in Christ, and walking in rebellion. The mental torment would flip me back between these thoughts, and finding myself remembering only the good times. When we were good, it was really great, but in those times, I never was being my authentic self. When I started to crave stepping back into being the person I knew God wanted me to be, things would get bad. And when they were bad, they were really bad.

During this mental battle, I needed to see clearly. I wrote down all the pros and cons of our relationship in my journal. Then, I wrote each circumstance I felt anxiety, fear, or just a sense of fight or flight on sticky notes. I decided to put these notes on my bathroom mirror to reflect on every time I looked in the mirror. My entire bathroom mirror was filled with them. It was an attempt in myself to remember those times and not turn back. I wanted to remember the times he tried to force me to say I'm sorry, the times he told me "you're mine" or "you're whipped" while placing his hands around my throat, even if this was in a said "playful" manner. I wanted to remember the times he would raise his voice at me and yell, telling me I was crazy. Those were not who I was! That was not what I was going back to.

Crystal Pain

But after time, I realized that I was only concentrating on the negative. I was surrounding myself with the pain, and this was not how God wanted me to escape. He is light and not darkness. By concentrating on this darkness, I was still giving it power in my life.

"I am the light of the world. If you follow me, you won't have to walk in darkness, because you will have the light that leads to life" (John 8:12, NLT).

I was allowing unforgiveness to take root and hold place. I had forgotten that my battle was not with a person. I was to be a carrier of light. So, I removed all these notes and replaced them with the words of God. I wrote down who God said I was, the love He has for me, and His grace in our lives. In doing this, I was gaining confidence and clarity. I was starting to grab hold of His truth over myself again.

"And you will know the truth, and the truth will set you free" (John 8:32, NLT).

It was not my job to be concerned with how my ex chose to view things, but only my job to take responsibility for what I was doing. He'd say I did him wrong and that I would always battle between two different people, and one just didn't like him. He said that he forgave me for everything "I" did and said he was sorry for not being "good enough" for me. I was upset that he never saw any other issues. That he wasn't able to see the depth of the struggles we had. But at this time, I wasn't going to try and explain anything else. If he and I needed to be together, I felt God would have to reveal these things to him. If they never were, then that's okay. I was starting fresh. I was done with the cycle, the ride on the merry-go-round. I was determined to break free and seek God's truth. It was going to require me to be able to accept God's truth and cast down anything that challenged it.

My ex would say something that showed a glimpse of truly

loving me. If I didn't respond, it was always followed with a horrible insult. These were the hardest to overcome. I understood the insult was probably his protective reaction to feeling rejected by my silence. I will use one of his comments during these reactive moments to highlight a place I commonly got stuck. He made a comment that I sickened him and made fun of the fact I was a widow. He told me that I was posting selfies with words on Facebook about God while making videos on TikTok for guys' attention. This hurt my heart so badly. I allowed him to completely slice me in half with his tongue. What I was actually doing was idolizing his opinions of me over God's.

This was Satan using accusations against me. I had openly revealed all my weaknesses to my ex. So, Satan knew exactly how to use him to hit me where it hurt. Satan will often make truthful statements and twist them around to use them against us. While Jesus was in the wilderness, exhausted from not eating for forty days, Satan tried this technique on Jesus. By taking Him to the holy city and quoting the scriptures out of context, and twisting them around, he tried to get Jesus to doubt His identity. Satan gets us to partner with these accusations because they contain some truth. It's that portion of truth within the statements that cause us to hold on to them longer than we need. In doing this, we can start to struggle with questioning ourselves. We question our identity in Christ and who He says we are. As for me, that identity had become blurred by my own shame of living in rebellion and easily laying it down. I also had not been feeding on His Word and resting in His presence. Like Jesus, after fasting for forty days, I was exhausted and had grown weary. Jesus was strong and able to combat these attacks with the truth of God's Word. I needed to realize that Jesus was there, too, with me in this wilderness. He would also come alongside me in combating the enemy and guide me to His truth.

I knew that the statements my ex was saying carried some truth

Crystal Pain

but needed Jesus to show where they were twisted in the delivery. I had been double-minded and highly aware of the fact that I had been battling between two different people. The truth was, I knew who I was in Christ. I had made a conscious decision to lay down my rebellious nature. I knew nothing else would satisfy me like Jesus. By this time, with His grace, I had already been wholeheartedly following Him for several months. I was a widow, and walking through this journey where I felt most misunderstood by others. It was an area that caused me to think I didn't fit in with anyone anymore. God's truth was, He had confirmed that my grief journey would be used for His testimony. I had posted words on Facebook often and previously struggled with doubting that I heard God's voice and was called to share His gospel. Again, I had to reflect on His truth. God tells us His sheep hear His voice, and He has called us all to share the good news. My daughter made a video on TikTok with me in it. I thought while doing this, I was too old. The truth was, I wasn't doing this for the attention of men. I had prayed that God continue to grow my daughter and my relationship, and this was evidence of that.

I had a choice to make and to seek God on who He said I was. None of the comments my ex was saying could make me doubt my identity, as long as I accepted and held on tight to the person deep down inside me that I knew I was. God reminded me I didn't have to defend myself. In those things he was pointing out, I had to understand that my ex was reacting out of confusion and hurt too. He might have been retaliating, but what I was fighting was the spirit behind them. I needed to refuse to argue with it and only hold on to God's truth over my life. I knew that God had never left me through this entire pit I found myself in. He was constant in wooing me and showing things that He developed my foundation on. My heart had been purified through Him. And anything that I had done, once repented of, was nailed to the cross with Jesus. I had to refuse to wear any name that God did not assign. I knew anything

Crystal Pain of the Spiritual War

He brought me through, He placed a purpose for my future on it.

I needed to speak out against these spirits and realize that if negative emotions were surfacing, those were areas that I still needed to submit to God. However, I did not stand up to them. I chose to run and hide. I battled with doubt and was unstable. I allowed fear to control me in these times and was relearning how to stand firm in the power God extended through His love and mercy. I did not face them in prayer, front and center. There was still discipline and training I had to redevelop. I needed to regain an understanding of what partnering with God looked like.

As time went on, my ex started to contact my daughter and even sent her a video that was posted ten years ago when she was around eight years old. I thought, *More than likely, he was struggling without the ability to make sense of everything.* My daughter had gotten to know him over the past few years, but she felt uncomfortable with this. She came to me, saying, "Mom, this has gotten to be just weird." I hated that she was brought into it and hated that my errors had caused her to be uncomfortable. My daughter is the one area that I will fight like no other for.

After about three months, I ran into him at the gym and tried to ignore him. He ended up coming up to me while I was on the ground doing an abdominal workout. Even though I felt that I was in an inferior position physically on the ground, I wouldn't speak to him. He got irritated and yelled at me. He said I was sick and needed help, then threatened he would get my daughter involved. I tried not to say anything but was so filled with terror. I filed a complaint with the gym. He drove off in anger and then came back to the gym and parked outside, waiting. I wouldn't leave the gym until I saw him finally drive off for good. Eventually, I went to the sheriff's office and filed stalking charges.

I was so afraid of the repercussions of this, even though they informed me I had more than enough evidence for these charges

Crystal Pain

to be placed. I went to them several times before officially filing a report. Even though they were convinced of my need to do so, they told me stalking is any unwanted contact that continues to go on. I honestly didn't want it to go like this. I had already gotten so far down this road. I just wanted it to all end. After this, I would shake uncontrollably just seeing his vehicle. Even if it wasn't his car, if I saw a vehicle that was the same make and model, my heart started pounding. I knew that this was more to do with me stepping away from a lifestyle than a person. But I lost control of regulating that fear.

There were times that I was terrified for my life, and I would start trembling. I was not sure if I was afraid of him, but fear consumed me nonetheless. I was hiding and not wanting to leave my house. I often felt like there was someone always watching me. I cut off communication with almost everyone most days. I had been feeling totally misunderstood and in a sort of torment I couldn't explain in words. I kept a gun on my nightstand, thinking every creek in my house was an intruder coming in. Fear gripped me, and I some days couldn't stop crying. I stayed in bed for days at a time, so depressed I couldn't get out. I even, at one point, battled suicidal thoughts like it was an actual person talking to me. I was bound to something and needed help.

One Sunday at my church, two of our pastors called for anyone that felt bound by something to come forward for prayer. I battled, walking forward. After all, I had already been prayed for by my friend, Cami, months back and felt a breaking. I thought I should already be free from this. I also was battling to humble myself. This was my church, one I attended for twenty years and at one time served on multiple platforms. I even worked for them for three years. How embarrassing to be the one who had backslid and now found myself in bondage to the very things I used to live my life setting others free from. I was wearing the label prodigal like a scarlet letter. But I knew I needed deliverance; I also knew there

Crystal Pain of the Spiritual War

were still areas of my life I hadn't placed back on the altar and repented of. I finally walked forward. I found myself on the ground quickly. I was gripping the ground, moaning, shaking, and manifesting as something broke its grip on me. Laying there in a puddle of snot and tears, a sister in Christ came to me and sat down on the ground with me and just held me. Feeling that love of the Father through her was unexplainable. Knowing that there was something evil that had attached itself to me, yet she was still willing to hold me and see me as God's child, spoke volumes to me.

There were layers of breaking free from this spiritual attack, and it wasn't something that I could do alone. It required a community of believers, brothers and sisters that were there to come alongside me and walk it out with me. This particular sister was trained in inner healing and, in the weeks to follow, walked me through depths of recognizing entry points and doors I had open to the enemy.

I now visibly recognized the battle I had been in and knew I had been fighting some major spiritual warfare. Again, God tells us that our war is not against flesh and blood but against the principalities of darkness. I was able to differentiate between the people in my story and the spirits making the attack behind it. I think often the actual person is innocent, and what we truly are fighting is just the manifestation of a demonic spirit. More than likely, the person in our story has also withstood trauma in their life and has been fighting their own battle. They, too, were just being used to play a role in our battle, and Satan found a way to innocently use them.

We are not to lash out at the person in the flesh, hold bitterness in our hearts toward another, seek revenge, or get to a place of unforgiveness. Our hearts should always be to see others step into freedom and walk in the fullness of who God desires them to become. There is an old saying holding on to bitterness is like drinking poison and expecting the other person to get sick. Holding on to bitterness, envy, hate, or anger can make your body sick and damage you. Unforgiveness can block your healing from these sicknesses, as well as prevent you from being set free from Satan's schemes.

"When you forgive this man, I forgive him, too. And when I forgive whatever needs to be forgiven, I do so with Christ's authority for your benefit, so that Satan will not outsmart us. For we are familiar with his evil schemes" (2 Corinthians 2:10, NLT).

You must realize that this type of attack needs to be addressed through prayer. It is done in the spirit realm. You don't do the battling. You are powerless without God. The battle belongs to HIM. Our job is to repent, release, and submit to Him. We are to invite Him into these areas. We must allow the Holy Spirit to open our eyes to the areas broken, to the wounds we have tried in ourselves to heal, and say, "Come, Father! I release my control; I see my attempts to change without your grace. I want to do it your way. Show me your way."

> *It is true, we live in a body of flesh. But we do not fight like people of the world. We do not use those things to fight with that the world uses. We use the things God gives to fight with, and they have power. Those things God gives to fight with destroy the strong places of the devil. We break down every thought and proud thing that puts itself up against the wisdom of God. We take hold of every thought and make it obey Christ.*

2 Corinthians 10:3–5 (NLV)

It states, "Every thought and PROUD thing that puts itself up against the wisdom of God." Did you catch that part? Recognizing

Crystal Pain of the Spiritual War

and handling pride is a HUGE key to our healing and receiving ultimate freedom. I want you to tuck this truth away in your pocket and consciously reflect on that as you continue to read.

CHAPTER 6

CRYSTAL PAIN OF RECOGNIZING THE NARCISSISTIC SPIRITS

By now, I was aware that I was in a spiritual battle and desperately seeking the guidance of the Holy Spirit. I was determined to submit to Him and allow Him to show me both what was attacking me, why I was a target, and how I opened doors to give it this permission. I also wanted to remember that what I was battling was not a person. This was a time in our society when the discussion on narcissism was really being highlighted. I touched on this earlier and explained how I believe that the pandemic created an incubation period for self-focus to mature in stature. Naturally, I gravitated toward studying narcissistic personality disorder. I do not think that everyone who displays selfishness has this disorder per se, but I had a strong conviction about the distinct character traits that were associated with it.

I began to study these traits and find out where in the scriptures I could find them in operation. I was led to 1 Kings and the story of Jezebel, Ahab, and the prophet Elijah. After examining these passages, I believe God revealed a correlation between what is referred to today as narcissistic abuse and the cluster of spirits

Crystal Pain

working together as a team throughout this story. I knew that in the spirit realm, demons operate like an army with rankings and a dispatch system, and there is often a leader or strongman that is in charge over other lesser-ranked spirits. It is in Ephesians 6:12 that it is stated that our war is not against flesh and blood. It separately describes that our war is against leaders, powers, and spirits of darkness.

In this story, Jezebel was the wife of King Ahab. Ahab was referred to as the king that did more evil in the sight of the Lord than any other king prior to him. This reference was because Ahab originally came from a Godly background but rebelled against this and sacrificed these Godly behaviors and worshipped the false god, Baal. He did this to bow down to his wife, Jezebel. Jezebel would often set out and accomplish tasks for Ahab that satisfied his fleshly desires. We see an example of this when Ahab wanted to possess a vineyard that belonged to a man named Naboth. When Naboth would not sell it to him, Ahab went home, went to bed sulking, and refused to eat. This vineyard that belonged to Naboth was a family inheritance. He refused to trade or sell his generational blessing. Jezebel asked why Ahab was upset, and after he told her, she said, "I will get you what you want." She orchestrated a plan. She forged papers in King Ahab's name, using His power (given to him by God), and tricked the townspeople into having Naboth killed. Jezebel was full of pride and anger, controlling, manipulative, and destroyed anything that got in the way of what she wanted. She worshipped idols, convinced others to do forbidden practices against the Lord's ways, and set out to silence the voice of God. We see in this story an attack she plotted against the prophet Elijah. Ahab was no better because he allowed all of this. He was only focused on obtaining his fleshly desires.

There are similarities in the destructive and selfish ways at work in the narcissistic movement we see discussed today. While I do not believe the "ghost" of Jezebel and Ahab are roaming around

Crystal Pain of Recognizing the Narcissistic Spirits

haunting us after their death. You will see distinct traits line up almost exactly with what is referenced by many claiming to experience narcissism. Some of these characteristics include seduction, control, victim mindsets, revenge, anger, murder, and wanting to silence God's voice. The demons and spirits that were in operation behind these people are still roaming around, looking for their next victim.

"When the unclean spirit is gone out of a man, he walketh through dry places, seeking rest, and findeth none. Then he saith, I will return into my house from whence I came out; and when he is come, he findeth it empty, swept, and garnished. Then goeth he, and taketh with himself seven other spirits more wicked than himself, and they enter in and dwell there: and the last state of that man is worse than the first. Even so shall it be also unto this wicked generation" (Matthew 12:43–45).

I believe this proves these spirits roam around looking for a home that is swept clean, a new army base for lack of better terms. It's a place they can bring their entire team into. I believe that we, as Spirit-filled believers, cannot be possessed by them. After all, the word "possession" denotes ownership. God stripped Satan of all power and dominion. He owns nothing. However, we can open ourselves up to being oppressed. This means they attach to our souls and can influence us in areas we give them that authority. We need to be aware of those areas we have swept our house clean and have our eyes open to them. We leave our house (our soul) swept clean when we remove Godly principles and foundational beliefs from our lives. We need to remember our battle is not with people but with these spiritual entities trying to gain control over us. There is great power in recognizing them, understanding their schemes, and seeing the access points. We need to see the doors that are opened to give them rule and reign in others' lives or through us. Once you see the entryways, remember God already stripped them of power and dominion. We then just give God the

Crystal Pain

green light through repentance to close the door as easily as it was opened and receive the key to lock it shut for good. That key is His truth and reinstating it within the foundational ways we choose to operate.

I believe in this study, God showed me similarities behind the evil at work in Jezebel and Ahab and those same evil spirits working in the narcissistic movement we see today. I truly believe that the spirits behind Jezebel and Ahab work under the leadership of the Leviathan Spirit (the Master of Pride). They are still trying to silence the works of God in our lives and manipulate situations to satisfy fleshly desires. They want to turn our focus on self, what we want, and what we think we deserve. They make us believe that there is nothing wrong with obtaining it by any means necessary. They trick us into placing other things as idols in our lives over God.

There are distinct traits that are associated with what I'll refer to as the Spirit of Jezebel and those that are associated with the Ahab Spirit. However, you will always see them working together. One cannot operate without the cooperation of the other. They both desire power and control through manipulation. They seek to obtain the blessings God has passed down generationally by getting you to trade or replace them with something else. There are differentiations in how they set out to accomplish this. Jezebel gains dominance through seduction, flattery, trickery, and twisting the truth. It will destroy anything that gets in its way when challenged, especially God. Ahab portrays a submissive nature but uses weakness and victim status to get others to side with it and ultimately do its dirty work. It might have a position of authority but easily extends its power to others if it can gain benefit in doing so. It will often show cowardly character and emotionally crumble when caught. It operates behind the scenes by not standing up for things that are right and going along with evil schemes.

Crystal Pain of Recognizing the Narcissistic Spirits

Although I have spent years studying inner healing and demonic influence, I'm not an expert in demonology, nor do I want to be. I want to spend more of my focus on the goodness and power of God's love. When Job was in the pit of his greatest trial, God mentioned the Leviathan. And He asks him who he thinks he is to think he is mighty enough to come up against the monster called Leviathan. You see, we aren't called to slay all these demons, but what we are called to do is submit under the powerful love of God and let Him wash us clean. God created us in His image, and we need to recognize those things that are not lining up with that image and allow Him to transform us with His love. We are called to resist temptation. Once you (working with God) rid yourself of anything you have in common with these spirits, it is then they lose access to any control over you. In Job's case, he had an open door through fear. He even mentions that the thing he feared the most has come upon him.

"What I was afraid of has come upon me. What filled me with fear has happened" (Job 3:25, NLV).

Fear and faith operate quite parallel. I like the saying "If you have a lot of fear, you actually operate with a high level of faith." You've just placed its power in the wrong kingdom. On top of being fearful, Job was spiritually arrogant as well. Yes, he was a beautiful man of God, but he, too, wasn't absent of needing refining. He questioned God. Because he was doing everything that had ever been asked of him, he felt God had no reason to allow such things to happen to him.

Have you ever found yourself here? Saying, "God, I lived a good life. Why are you allowing this?" Or maybe saying, "I corrected the situation and did what you asked, and you still haven't blessed me." Or maybe it's, "Why do bad things always happen to good people?"

God had to rebuke Job and remind Job of the position God was

Crystal Pain

to hold in His life. No circumstance we encounter changes God's position of power. Are you truly willing to lay down your life to God, ready to give up total control? You see, Job had developed some pride in himself. Suffering can often reveal the deepest part of our self-focus. It can reveal those settled developments in our good doings that implant a desire for merit, praise, blessings, or admiration. Once Job repented of all this, he received back what he had lost and was even blessed greater than before.

There was a spirit in operation being used against Job. It was Leviathan, mentioned in Job 41. Leviathan is known in theology as the "King over all the Children of Pride." Have you ever stopped to think about who those children might be and if our eyes are open to how they have fixated themselves into our own lives? It's easy to find yourself in the middle of a narcissistic battle (which is ruled by Leviathan and works with a team of other spirits or "children") and want to scream at the top of your lungs how horrible it was. There is a yearning to point a finger at a particular person and highlight everything they did to you. You might want to reveal every evil thing you believe they caused. I understand doing this out of the heart to warn others or prevent them from getting hurt. But I would like to take this a little deeper, to a place that will prevent ever attracting this type of toxicity again. It will require something very difficult. It was for me, anyway. What I am referring to is how hard it was to look at myself and ask myself, do I have anything in common with them? Did I play a role in this attack? Where did I not recognize the open doors that allowed it control?

One of the most common things you will find with narcissistic abuse victims is that they, at some time or another, ask themselves, "Am I the narcissist?" I believe this is partially because these are people who often experience great trauma in their life. That trauma might have been fresh when they met their claimed abuser. Maybe it was from their childhood. Those wounds are access points, the open doors. These unhealed areas we must place under

Crystal Pain of Recognizing the Narcissistic Spirits

God's love. Looking from another angle, I wonder if the reason the question "Am I the narcissist?" is asked has something to do with God's leading. He wants His people to recognize if they have any similarities within themselves or something that was partnering with the spirits guiding the attacks. He desires those things to be brought to Him. Then we repent and say, "Rid me of this." We give Him access to shut that open door. Again, this strips the enemy from control.

You see, the biggest tool this army of spirits uses is pride. In a person who is diagnosed with NPD (narcissistic personality disorder), you see huge egos, unable to accept they are ever at fault, the judgment of others, thinking someone else took something that should have been theirs, flipping blame on others, or even devaluing someone else that they see advancing. There are many other characteristics that stem from them, but the root of them all is pride. It's pride that comes in through a wounded soul. They have partnered with the lie that they deserve the highest respect. They deserve praise because they never got it, or they are special and have been unfairly overlooked. Again, it's a root of pride.

"Every thought and PROUD thing that puts itself up against the wisdom of God." (Do you still have this in your pocket?)

The truth is, you can't control someone else's healing. You can't change someone that isn't ready to see where there needs to be change. I'm not negating the fact one can experience true hurt from these attacks, but the only thing you can do is submit yourself to God and allow Him to heal and change you. Change YOU? Yes, you guessed it, I want to flip the script.

CHAPTER 7

CRYSTAL PAIN OF FLANKING

One of the most common things I have seen in my grief journey is patterns. You will even recognize these patterns while reading this very book. God will, each year, show me an area that He wants to come into. Each year we seem to revisit that area and go deeper into the healing process. Trauma can often open old wounds we have deep down inside us. Our temptation is to partner with despair. I'm not just referring to a poor-me mindset, although that is a first thought. It is easy to get to that place. Having something precious stripped away from you, something that you dreamed of and worked years to grow and develop, is an excruciating pain. I'm wanting to talk about something that we actually get tethered to and find ourselves unable to break free from.

God can and wants to use all things we endure to bring even more wisdom, growth, and freedom. Just like with Job, He wants to totally encompass our hearts and souls to bring even greater blessings into our lives, as well as use us to be blessings for others and the growth of His kingdom. He wants to pour out so much on and through you but must make sure that your character and foundation can handle the weight. We need to make room for these blessings.

Crystal Pain

I can't help but think, He sees something so great in us that He uses the worst of encounters to cut deep down in our souls and do supernatural surgery. He goes one layer at a time as the healing progresses. It's part of that etching the Master Craftsman is doing in creating you into a one-of-a-kind masterpiece. You just have to ask yourself how badly you want to be transformed into the person in this next season that He desires you to be. Are you ready to become the person He originally destined you to be while you were still in your mother's womb? What that is going to require of you is facing yourself. It will require facing pride and the idols that you have placed above His glory and power.

The enemy doesn't fight fairly. He will often use a flank maneuver. This is a military term used in battle where an opponent uses a simultaneous attack from two different sides in hopes of rendering their challenger hopelessly defeated. You see, often with narcissist relationships, people describe themselves as being left feeling destroyed. There was a death to their ability to see who they were in Christ, a distortion of the vision He had over their life, and their self-esteem was shattered. This is one of Satan's main goals with the use of the Jezebel and Ahab Spirits.

It's easy to see the error in others' behaviors and how they are mistreating you. You might have seen with clarity the dominating control, the unleashing of attacks to destroy each other physically or verbally. Often people experienced the seduction and flattery that enables guards to come down just before experiencing these blows. Terror, anxiety, and the weight of carrying blame for everything wrong in the relationship are strongly felt.

Remember, this is a flanking maneuver. There are two different sides that are used against you in the spirit realm. These attacks are not coming from a person in flesh in blood, but they are coming from two high-ranking forces in Satan's army used against you. There needs to be an awareness of both sides of this attack and how they execute their plans in totality. Jezebel Spirit influences someone to become seductive, dominating, and a ruthless destroyer. It whispers to not let anything stop them from gaining the things they feel they deserve. On the opposite side of that is the Ahab Spirit. They work in tandem together. Ahab influences someone to be submissive and use a victim status to justify doing wrong or to get others to do things for them. It is cowardly. The evilest thing is it uses those that know what is right by convincing them to refuse to stand up for it. I believe both spirits can flow in and out of a narcissistic relationship. I also believe that both parties in the relationship have a responsibility to recognize if and when they are coming into agreement with either one of these spiritual entities.

It requires laying down your pride. You must be humble enough to look deep inside your own soul and not just focus on said perpetrator. If you skip this step, you are only leaving yourself open for a repeat attack. I had to ask myself, do I have any voids in my soul that I left uncovered by the Lord? Have I allowed these areas to develop into anything that has caused me to operate in an unhealthy manner? Is there anything to this behavior that seems out of control, something that could be described as tormenting my everyday thoughts? Have I developed an unnatural level of rebellion, anger, hate, self-focus, pride, pity, jealousy, fear, or resentment that is overpowering at times?

I do believe that everyone, at some time or another, deals with self-focus and can be narcissistic at times. We are human, and dying to our flesh is a daily walk. We all have areas that we struggle with and are works in progress. Especially when you are freshly walking out of a grieving process. If you surround yourself with relationships that are walking a lifestyle sold out to God, you will easily be able to put a stop to these behaviors. You will find that on both sides, you are able to give and receive accountability when these spirits try to nudge their way in. It's when you leave these unattended and give them reign to fully gain access that they can

Crystal Pain

steadily grow in their influence over your lives. Ultimately, they then end up destroying both parties in the relationship, which is Satan's goal.

"The thief's purpose is to steal and kill and destroy" (John 10:10, NLT).

I am talking about feeling like something has become such a burden it's tormenting and won't relent. You can't even recognize who you are anymore. As for me, I could sense and feel demonic activity. I even saw these spirits early on. I didn't recognize who I was at all anymore. I refused to do anything to stop it. Eventually, though, I became so sensitive to feeling the malevolence developing around me became unbearable for me, and I just fled. I got so deep in confusion that it took months for me to recognize what was happening and where I allowed it access.

After removing myself from the situation, I had to realize it was not my job to control anyone else, but I was responsible for the areas in my own soul that I left unsubmitted to God. I needed to become aware of those places within my own actions that I was allowing pride and my desire to control permission to operate. Again, I am not negating the fact that there was true pain, fear, abuse, or absolute confusion. I admit there was a part of me that wanted to be the victim in this. What I was experiencing was real. I first found myself praying daily that God would heal my ex, and reveal Himself in a powerful and tangible way that would bring my ex great revelation of all the things he was doing wrong. I wanted more than anything to write this off as just being in a narcissistic relationship and diagnose my ex as being the narcissist. It was simple for me to see that narcissism lined up quite parallel to the workings of Jezebel and Ahab when I read about them in the scriptures. It would have been easy to just walk away saying my ex was the narcissist and an evil person.

That is what Satan wants us to do. He desires to turn us against

Crystal Pain of Flanking

one another and use our strength to conduct his plan of destroying people. He wants us to focus on a person and retaliate against them. We must be able to separate a person, including ourselves, from a sin. We were created from the foundation of the earth as saints before Him, His sons and daughters. Sin separates us from Him, and even after we are saved, we still encounter things we will have to overcome, but we can't forget who we are at the core. If Satan can keep us trapped in the victim mindset, we can end up allowing bitterness to take root inside us. That bitterness can cause defilement.

"See to it that no one falls short of the grace of God and that no bitter root grows up to cause trouble and defile many" (Hebrews 12:15, NIV).

Remaining bitter allows Satan to still have a foothold. If we choose to allow this bitterness to remain, it births unforgiveness. We can find ourselves meditating on the situation and keeping a record of wrongs. This is when we know that unforgiveness has transformed into resentment. If we let that simmer too long, then we step into retaliation. Retaliation builds into anger, hate, and, finally, violence. This may sound too far-fetched, but unfortunately, many have gotten to this point. It's that place where you say you're going to feel, experience, or hear my pain. I was not going to give power to evil by remaining unforgiveness. I was turning over my wounds to God and exchanging them for wisdom and God's true freedom. The moment I walked away from that relationship, I placed my ex in God's hands. I needed to leave it in God's hands and stop picking it back up. You can't keep looking in your rearview mirror and remain focused on the road God has placed in front of you.

I had to identify how in my story, these spirits were working as a team. I decided to turn my focus to myself and allow the Holy Spirit to reveal the areas within this spiritual war that I had

Crystal Pain

given authority to the enemy and allowed him to influence my beliefs and behaviors. I needed to understand that, through repentance and humility, God could restore me with the strength to say no to following their leadership and turn from these habits. I was determined to discover these areas, to repent, to renounce my partnership with them, and to turn authority back over to God. I knew He would bring deliverance to me. I knew once I rid myself of the things I had in common with these spirits; all torment would seize.

It was tempting to take up offense. There was a struggle I underwent; please know I am not insinuating that everyone who goes through these attacks is under my same conviction. I am merely sharing my experience. For myself, I found myself saying to God, "You don't know what I have been through," "You don't understand how much the pain I endured wore me down," "I am tired of fighting; I'm exhausted." I had closed Him out early in my grief journey; I had forgotten He not only knew me more than anyone on earth, but in yoking myself to Him, He gave great authority and power. I just neglected to use it.

When Satan found me, like Ahab, I was in a rebellion against God's call on my life. I had sacrificed Godly behaviors out of anger, confusion, and want to just live my life for my own selfish gain. I found myself once again rejecting the things I knew God had called me to. I placed other things above God as idols and appraised their opinions of me as higher than God's. My background was godly, but I laid that all down to satisfy my flesh. By doing this, I swept my house clean and opened myself up to be influenced by these spirits. I even found myself sulking, not getting out of bed, and even not eating. Although there was an initial grieving period I needed to undergo after, I had allowed a victim mindset to take root, and hopelessness overshadowed God's truth that I was more than a conqueror. I didn't hold on to the truth that God is strong in my weaknesses and will work everything together for my good. This kept me in the wilderness longer than I needed to be.

Crystal Pain of Flanking

In this, God showed me an area that was not just rebellious anger. I had already repented of partnering with rebellion and been set free from that. There was a subtle form of Pride at work. It was even hard for me to acknowledge I was operating in it. Much of society has deemed this underlying trait as acceptable, which gave much disguise to it. There were facts attached to my story that gave me, according to society, permission to feel this form of pride. I left my soul unsupervised and unsubmitted to the healing of the Holy Spirit for so long that this pride outgrew all other forms at work. In doing this, I opened myself up to being under the influence of this form of pride. I was actively partnering with more than just a mindset now. It was tormenting. There was a Spirit at work with me. I could justify it, share it, and receive attention by expressing it. The spirit started to feed off the power it received from others' recognition. This spirit at work was self-pity. I believe this is one of the greatest areas we can find ourselves in distortion and start resembling the characteristics of the Ahab Spirit.

It was time its ringleader, "Leviathan," the Master of All Pride, lost its grip. It was time to expose all mechanisms of Jezebel and Ahab and refuse partnership with both of them. It was time to place God back on the throne and give Him rule over my life again. When we walk in complete humility before the Lord, He rescues us.

"Humble yourself before the Lord and he will lift you up in honor" (James 4:10, NLT).

Humility is not something God gives us; it is something we must choose. He can use situations in our life that lead us to this choice, but it is ultimately our decision. Once we humble ourselves, die to the pride in us, and submit, He can flow in our lives as our rescuer. I knew it was time that the battle ended, and I was filled back up, no longer exhausted and striving. But full of joy! His joy! Our Father was there, reaching His hand out to me and

Crystal Pain

wanting to partner with me. I had to take intimate time with the Holy Spirit and allow Him to guide me through the examination of my soul and those areas I filled with various forms of pride. He is the Great Physician. Just like a physical physician sits with you, takes ex-rays of areas you can't see with the natural eye, and explains the healing steps; the Great Physician (the Holy Spirit) did the same. He only required my humility, trust, and full submission to His love.

If you haven't slammed the pages of this chapter shut yet, thank you for the opportunity to explain in more depth what and how the Spirit of Self-Pity attacked and how it disguised itself in my story. I hope you see how its role is to get you to open a door and enable the Jezebel and Ahab Spirits to come in and attempt to destroy your life. I hope to show how they all worked together within my story by setting out to destroy more than just myself. I can't express enough that it isn't something we fight, but God does the battling. Recognition, repentance, and submission are our job. Invite the Father into that place and let Him do His work.

We see in the story of Elijah that after he took on Jezebel and Ahab, his life was threatened, and he became so afraid he fled. At one point, he told the Lord that he wanted him to take his life. He actually said, "I've had enough, LORD. Take my life!" Have you been here? I know I encountered suicidal thoughts.

As Elijah was hiding, God did not scorn him, but He allowed him to rest and fed him. God will do the same for us. He isn't a scornful God punishing us. When we need rest, He provides it. He will do the same for us, just as He did for Elijah. However, don't forget that He did make Elijah reflect on the reason he was hiding and eventually challenged him to get up! I know God wants us all to "Get Up" and not partner with this fear and pride that causes us to want to end our lives. What causes us to give up? For myself, it was the tag team of spirits under the operation of the Leviathan

80

Crystal Pain of Flanking

"King of the Children of Pride." It was the flanking attacks I experienced from the spirits of Jezebel and Ahab. That feeling of being double-minded and confused, a fog of sorts, came over me. That shaking, I felt, was a test of my faith. I believe it is what God was showing us in James 1. I had to trust in this testing that God is at work.

> *Consider it nothing but joy, my brothers and sisters, whenever you fall into various trials. Be assured that the testing of your faith [through experience] produces endurance [leading to spiritual maturity, and inner peace]. And let endurance have its perfect result and do a thorough work, so that you may be perfect and completely developed [in your faith], lacking in nothing. If any of you lacks wisdom [to guide him through a decision or circumstance], he is to ask of [our benevolent] God, who gives to everyone generously and without rebuke or blame, and it will be given to him. But he must ask [for wisdom] in faith, without doubting [God's willingness to help], for the one who doubts is like a billowing surge of the sea that is blown about and tossed by the wind. For such a person ought not to think or expect that he will receive anything [at all] from the Lord, being a double-minded man, unstable and restless in all his ways [in everything he thinks, feels, or decides]. Let the brother in humble circumstances glory in his high position [as a born again believer called to the true riches and to be an heir of God]; and the rich man is to glory in being humbled [by trials revealing human frailty, knowing true riches are found in the grace of God], for like the flower of the grass he will pass away. For the sun rises with a scorching wind and withers*

Crystal Pain

the grass; its flower falls off and its beauty fades away; so too will the rich man, in the midst of his pursuits, fade away blessed [happy, spiritually prosperous, favored by God] is the man who is steadfast under trial and perseveres when tempted; for when he has passed the test and been approved, he will receive the [victor's] crown of life which the Lord has promised to those who love Him.

James 1:2–12 (AMPC)

What a beautiful promise! I want to not walk in doubt. I want to grow in wisdom, I want to walk in humility and receive the promise. I want the ability to wear the victor's crown with strength and dignity. Again, I can only reference with certainty the ways I have witnessed myself partnering with the Jezebel and Ahab Spirits. Again, my journey and reactions are not a direct, all-encompassing list of ways these spirits can attack. I share my experience in hopes of bringing awareness to anyone else that feels they are under unrelenting torment. Especially if you find yourself coming out of a battle with narcissism directly after you experienced trauma or loss of any kind. I do not want these attacks to be recurring in my life or anyone else's life.

I found myself in one battle after another, thinking that freedom was right around the corner. I remember saying, "God, you said if I do this or that, then I will be free. But I am still experiencing torment. Why?"

I had just been asking the Lord this question when He brought to my remembrance a dream I had several months prior to walking away from this spiritual attack.

I was at the church and had been placed in charge of organizing the luggage for the mission team that was about to be sent out. I was trying to put everything in my little car, but it wouldn't fit. I

Crystal Pain of Flanking

kept saying if only I had a truck, it would make this a lot easier. As I struggled more and more, I just found myself exhausted and needing to take a nap in the middle of such a menial task. My eyes were so heavy I couldn't keep them open. I was in the middle of a circular bar where the mission team was sitting around waiting for me to finish the task, but I couldn't do it. I ran out of the foyer to the restroom. I was so frustrated and felt defeated. As I was exiting the restroom, right in front of me was my ex. He was dressed in a Spiderman costume and pretending to shoot webs at me and laughing. I ran out the door, and even though there were not actually webs covering me (they were only pretend), I felt like I was trapped in them. I was terrified. I started to feel so defeated, having no power over the imaginary webs. I said that I couldn't do it. I didn't want to fight anymore and gave up. It was then I woke up.

While seeking the Holy Spirit's guidance in interpreting this dream, I realized that there had always been a call in my life to the mission field. That was revealed in my hunger to help those in the marketplace carry the baggage that they accumulated along their life's journey and the desire to get them to a place where they, too, could be used to help others in the world. But this hunger had become hindered. I felt like everyone was placing pressure on me to do something for them, and that weight was causing such a heaviness on me. I found time to physically rest and would feel refreshed. However, shortly after returning to attempt the dream placed inside me, I would be met with webs of confusion. I often felt scared and sorry for myself. I would just give up on the dream. God was trying to show me there was a spirit attacking me, trying to ensnare me. You notice that I knew that, in my own might, I wasn't big enough. I needed the help of a bigger vehicle or a bigger source to carry the luggage of others. What I needed was to humble myself and ask for Jesus's help and the help of my church community. But I had become so self-focused by the struggle I didn't even ask for help. I told myself everything depended on me.

Crystal Pain

I also blamed my ex, thinking he was preventing me, but the only thing that was being used by him wasn't even his true identity. It was a disguise that I was seeing and pretended webs. There was no true power behind what Satan was using. I couldn't decern the difference between flesh and blood and the spirit coming at me. It was just like I believed so many other lies Satan deposited in my life.

By God walking me through this dream, I started to understand the why behind the constant inability to break free from the torment of the Leviathan's webs. I share this with you, hopefully, to keep others from being trapped and ensnared by this Leviathan spirit. It's a spirit often referred to as a water monster, a python spirit, a twisting and tentacle-wrapping beast. The one that is the "King of all the Children of Pride." I hope to expose those children and a few of their ugly disguises. In sharing my story, I want to allow God to reveal these traps! So, if you find yourself in a familiar fight, you too can say, "I see it, God, COME!" He has called us to set the captives free! He will do that through us and use all things for good that Satan sent out to destroy us! Whether that is fears cousin (doubt), the attack of pride through others, or the pride deposited inside us.

There are several ways the Jezebel Spirit with the Ahab Spirit operate. For myself, I easily slipped back in partnership with them after the series of events that happened following the death of my husband. However, this was not the first encounter I had with them. This particular team is one I had partnered with off in on throughout my entire life. I especially recognized their use of self-pity as a door opener in my life. I recognized this resurfacing during the part of my journey I like to call "Re-discovering Who You Are."

CHAPTER 8

CRYSTAL PAIN OF RE-DISCOVERING WHO YOU ARE

There's a familiar step many walk through in their grief journey. It's that portion where you stop and ask yourself, *Who am I?* I know for me, after losing a spouse, I got tripped up here more than once. I saw a repeat visit to this very question. It was like it would circle back around every few months. You see, in multiple areas of the Bible, God references marriage as two becoming united as one flesh. My husband and I took these principles to heart and implemented them in our marriage. We realized that our souls were intertwined and that what one did was a direct reflection of the other. We grew together, served together, dreamed together, and included each other in every aspect of our lives. Outside of God, he became the biggest reference in identifying myself. We both worked at becoming the best we could be individually, knowing it would only strengthen our collaboration as a whole. However, we did realize that in the areas where one was weak, the other was strong, and vice versa. Of course, God's grace covered us. There is such a synergy that happens in marriage when two die to their own selfish ambitions and work together for a vision that is greater

Crystal Pain

than themselves. I know this is why marriages are so attacked by the enemy. He hates this example. When done properly, it's one of the closest examples of Christ's relationship to the church we can have.

After my husband's death, it took me a long time to let the dust settle before even conquering this question, gathering my thoughts, and getting back on track to being used for growing God's kingdom. Everything I put my hand to felt empty without my husband by my side. It felt like I wasn't giving it my all with the part of who I used to be missing in his absence. Not to mention the pain it caused, even attempting to do things we once did together. This even included ministry. I stepped away from all aspects of ministry. Doing it without him hurt too much.

I went through an extremely rebellious stage. I was, at that time, unknowingly angry at God. I rejected the life in front of me. I didn't want to start over, rebuild, and walk away from the life of my dreams. How could God do this to me? I had given Him everything I had and served Him with all my gifts. Things I had run from in the past, I not only accepted, but for the first time in my life, I had a partner who not only encouraged me but understood me. Sometimes, it even felt like he was more excited about God using what was inside me than I was. I was so confused.

You see, Satan lurks around, just waiting for us to enter a state of confusion. Confusion always precedes sin. If Satan finds an area of confusion that goes uncovered, he comes in, sprinkles lies in the concoction and mixes it together. It's like he's baking a loaf of bread and mixes confusion with a little twisted truth and then lets it sit. Those little lies are like yeast and just a little works through the entire batch of dough.

"Don't you know that when you allow even a little lie into your heart, it can permeate your entire belief system?" (Galatians 5:9, TPT)

Crystal Pain of Re-Discovering Who You Are

What were those lies I was believing? How was it so easy for me not to see them? The enemy isn't creative. He often reuses lies. Things he has told us in the past. When he finds us in a broken, confused state, he just reinserts them. This is why it was hard for me to recognize them quickly. They felt familiar to me, so I was more accepting of them as truth. After closer examination of them, I established that they were lies Satan had been trying to make me partner with my entire life.

You see, through Jesus, we have been given all authority over the attacks of the enemy. He has been defeated and knows this. He knows that the true power is in Jesus and that power freely flows through us when we accept Jesus Christ as our Lord and Savior. The only way Satan can get to us is to make us open up a door to give Him access to our soul and make us partner with darkness. One of the ways he does this is by getting us to focus on ourselves and making us question the goodness of God.

Did you know that Satanists themselves are individuals that simply follow a self-centered philosophy? Satan himself was kicked out of heaven because of Pride and has been using this as his main source of gaining control ever since. Pride gives birth to every source of sin.

We can easily see it in the stereotypical ego-driven person, but have you ever stopped to see the areas where pride enters your own thought processes? Let's use my life to examine the types of self-focus and pride I found myself partnering with.

The first lie I believed was that God always makes me walk the hard road, that nothing in my life would ever be easy, and I was constantly going to have to work for things others received effortlessly. I believed that I would never get to keep things because they were eventually going to be taken from me. And it didn't matter how hard I worked at being the best I could at them. Nothing lasted forever. Therefore, I told myself never to get too attached to

Crystal Pain

things. I decided to guard my heart and never fully give it away. This made me often concentrate on the weak areas in life more than the strong. My focal point had become the lie that if I could fix the weak areas, then whatever I possessed would have more stability.

I also became very independent and found that before I accepted anything, be it doctrine, a person, or even personal help. They had to first go through a proving process. I needed the doctrine backed up with facts, the person to show a track record of success, and someone that was offering to help to prove they weren't doing this out of obligation but a true heart to want to serve.

On the outside, I was portrayed as a very driven, independent self-starter. I was seen as one who never needed help, kept her circle small because she surrounded herself with only strong people, and was full of wisdom that you can accept because it had been earned through many trials I had walked through. This sounds like a respectable person, right? I mean, someone looked up to in society. But these were all masks of torment that I had left unsubmitted to God in my life.

These all stemmed from deceptions I joined hands with throughout my life. These deceptions made me self-focused, and I placed self-protective guards around me. My life was actually beautiful, and I was blessed growing up. I want to just show the tricky ways Satan showed up to deposit lies and the fact that it can happen to all of us. It doesn't even have to come from a huge traumatic event. There doesn't have to be abuse, trauma, or pain surrounding your life that causes you to erect these walls. We all are children of God, created with purpose and called to positively impact the world. That's enough for us to be hated by the enemy.

I personally started agreeing with the Spirit of Self-Pity early in my life. It came in through living under strict religious customs and a performance-driven mindset. It was something that told me that I had to perform or look a certain way to receive anything enjoyable in life. I believed that if I was the perfect student, I would be successful in life. Or that if I were the perfect Christian, I would receive God's blessing. I also believed that if I was the best athlete, I would gain popularity. It even transferred to how I physically looked. I believed if I was pretty and skinny, I would receive love. Everything began to revolve around the things I could obtain, and I fixed my focus on myself.

I believed if I didn't do something perfectly and messed up, I was a burden to everyone. Yes, they would be there to bail me out. But I should feel shame because it was my error that got me in the predicament to begin with, and all the troubles in my life were directly related to my failure. The Spirit of Self-Pity is one of the strongest forms of Pride. It's more than a "poor me" mindset. It's also more than a victim mindset. It's a combination of poor me and something that tells you I'm a victim of all the horrible things because I am such a disaster in life. One that, if left unattended, could establish thoughts that lead you to want to "unalive yourself." That's a checkmate for the enemy. Goal accomplished.

By getting you to believe that you, in yourself, are responsible for your life, he subtly removes the need for God. You start to believe that you are a creator. You believe that you can manifest things in your life outside the power of God. If they are good things, you did it all on your own. You can bask in the glory of your accomplishments. If bad things happen, then you must have been the reason. It makes you believe you aren't deserving of good things and wallow in the loss by saying, "I always have bad things happen. Why do I try?" or "I'm just never good enough."

I mentioned the workings of pride within a narcissistic attack and how Jezebel and Ahab work together. I explained that when the Jezebel Spirit operates, it sees anything that gets in the way of it obtaining things it wants or deserves as a perpetrator. The culprit

Crystal Pain

is usually external, and it will destroy anything that challenges it. It says you missed out on something because of someone else. In destroying that obstacle, it can then obtain all it craves. Ahab, on the other hand, says, I deserve this or that but am too weak in myself to get it. It says I missed out on something because of myself. It gives power to self-pity by making someone believe they can't do anything perfectly. It is weak, so needs to employ others to get what it wants. It eventually can get you in such a submissive state that you can't even determine what is best for yourself, and you turn over all power, conforming to other beliefs.

You can see the similarities here, right? Both take the focus off God being the all-powerful one, the creator, and source and place that power in the hands of man. It incorporates the worship and idolization of man's power, not God. It gets us to remove God from the throne and replace Him with man. This revelation really brought with it much conviction for me. I might not have united with these mindsets to do evil per se, but I could see how I was influenced to believe these strategies were an optional tool to help me climb the ladder of success in life. I was guilty of not fully submitting to God's power and will in my life. I many times exchanged it for ways that centered around my own will or what others told me.

One thing I don't want to do is make it seem like there is a demon in every bush. We shouldn't be walking in paranoia through everyday life. We don't need to give Satan more power than he actually has. The truth is, Satan has no power. Only what we extend to him. We should be spending most of our time with God and focused on His goodness and power over our lives. Be aware of the fruits of the Holy Spirit that are freely extended to us. He gives us love, joy, peace, patience, kindness, generosity, faithfulness, gentleness, and self-control.

"Fix your thoughts on what is true, and honorable, and right,

Crystal Pain of Re-Discovering Who You Are

and pure, and lovely, and admirable. Think about things that are excellent and worthy of praise" (Philippians 4:8, NLT).

If our walk is one with God at the center, these manipulative tactics of the enemy will be easily highlighted. There will be a part of our spirit inside us that discerns something opposite to how we are empowered to live. I'm only using my story to highlight areas I was blinded. Once these areas were recognized and brought to God. They easily lost their power in my life.

Prior to meeting my husband, I had walked through inner healing and overcame these mindsets, broke the partnership with these lies, and ended up living a beautiful life and marriage. After his death, the enemy once again saw the opportunity to get me to grab hold of these lies again. He once again saw me broken, isolated, scared, and confused. I know that if I were surrounded by community and reached out for the love of God through them, I would have avoided much of the pain I went through. My walk through the wilderness would have been way shorter if I hadn't sold out to pride and forgotten I was not a victim. I also would have seen where I picked up self-pity and planted it like a seed in my soul, allowing it to grow into a powerful force in my life's direction.

Nevertheless, our God is so gracious, so loving, and never left my side through a process of events that followed. I made many mistakes, but I experienced God bring in a deeper understanding of humility, His mercy, His grace, and most importantly, the need for community.

(See Journal Entry "The Acceptance Stage" on page 262)

I started re-reading books I had read in the past. Revisiting how God used them to guide me in revealing my strengths and spiritual gifts. I took many personality tests and spent a lot of time trying to rediscover who I was. I desired to see again the part that I brought to the "two become one" equation in my marriage.

Crystal Pain

This ended up being a part of my journey that I found a lot of enjoyment in. I have always loved taking personality tests and studying what makes others tick. My employees used to joke around with me about this. When I closed the store, they even bought me a parting gift that included a book filled with personality tests. They told me they bought that for me because they knew I'd miss making them take these tests, and they knew how much I liked them. It made me giggle because it was true.

I used to make them take tests often. It was my heart for them to see the areas they had strength and help them understand who they were. Of course, as a business owner, I wanted to make sure I was taking advantage of their strongest skills and placing them in the proper role that utilized these gifts to benefit the success of my company. However, I also wanted them to see their strengths for themselves. I deeply cared for each one of my employees. I wanted to play an active role in showing them the only thing required of them was to grow in the areas that came naturally to them. It was my job as a manager to bring someone alongside them that was strong in the areas they were weak. I wanted them to recognize how doing what they did best, working alongside another employee that was doing the same (in an area they were weaker), they would automatically start to see themselves growing as an individual and gleaning from the other employee's strengths. As time went on, they grew greatly in the areas they formerly saw as weaknesses. I would be so proud of them because I saw many surpass the knowledge I, as the store owner, possessed. They went on to become some of the greatest women I know to this day.

I did these things because I grew up all over the place when it came to understanding my strengths. I often found myself in my earlier years, conforming to whatever it was that someone else saw in me or asked of me. I didn't know what I liked or didn't like. I just conformed to others. I even picked up hobbies others liked. I spent much of my life just trying to find true joy because I didn't

Crystal Pain of Re-Discovering Who You Are

know how to be authentically who I was created to be. I also failed at a lot of things because you need passion for success. If the supply of passion behind your reason for doing something doesn't rest deep down inside of you, that supply is going to run dry. It will cause frustration because you don't have a natural source inside you. It needs to be like a spring-fed pool that is constantly flowing from inside yourself.

I would find myself attempting sports that I wasn't bad at but ended up quitting. I was so afraid of failure or disappointing someone else. Mainly, this was because I knew I didn't have the drive like others for it. I ran track because my brother was a track star, and I was pretty fast. I did well, won races often, made the varsity team, and made it to regional meets every year. But I quit after three years. I ran cross country; we took second place at the state meet. But I quit that after three years, as well. I played basketball for three years, with the same outcome.

By the time I was in college, I continued to struggle. This was the first time I got to choose what "I" wanted. I got to choose what to go to school for and what I wanted to do for a career for the rest of my life. I remember they made us take a test that helped determine what career fit us best. I initially chose nursing. I even got my associate's degree in nursing from our local junior college. I changed my major two other times. The second thing I decided I wanted to be was a mortician. I know, sounds odd for a teenage girl. Especially since there was no other person I had ever met in my life that was a mortician, and I was deathly afraid of ghosts. Finally, I remember someone saying to choose something that you think you'll enjoy doing for the rest of your life. I then chose to attend a local University and major in Advertising Journalism with a minor in Psychology. I wanted to become a copywriter and somehow write commercials and print ads for clients.

It was in this major that my fear of rejection reared its head. I

Crystal Pain

had to take an ad sales class. In this class, we were to memorize a script and train in overcoming objections. Part of that class required us to go around selling advertising space to the community, and if you didn't reach the quota set by the professor, you didn't pass. I dropped the class twice. I was great at presentations in class but terrified to speak to the actual business owners in the community. Rejection and fear of failure were enough to cripple me. I attempted two other careers to finally find myself in retail management. This came so naturally to me, and I advanced quickly in every company I worked for. Before the age of twenty-seven, I had already advanced to management or offered my own store by three different big box retail stores. I spent fifteen years in the retail management field.

As I have mentioned before, I opened and ran my own store for seven years. Prior to opening this store, God told me to use my skills in retail to reach the marketplace for Him. It took many years of preparation and wasn't an overnight thing, but God told me, "Take care of my people, and I will take care of you."

The store wasn't easy for me, but I never lost my passion for it. That passion was rooted in something deep down inside of me. It was the glory and hunger to see God's love touch others in ways I had hungered for that truth my whole life. I wanted to show my employees their value. I wanted to love on my customers and for them to know that when they came in my store, whatever heavy thing they were carrying, they could leave it at the feet of Jesus and walk out of there lighter. I wanted to partner with other non-profits monetarily and help change the community around us. God so graciously allowed me to do all these things through this business. The natural spring of passion inside of me came from the love and grace of the Holy Spirit flowing in me.

After my husband passed, my vision got blurry. As I discussed earlier. My spring was drying up because I lost the passion inside me. I was taking so much time trying to heal. I didn't know how to help others. My father passed away a year after my husband, and now I needed to help walk my mom through grief too. It was a big season of feeling lost.

I shut the store down, thinking I needed to stop. I needed to take time for myself to heal and be there for my mom. I needed a fresh start and a fresh vision. I needed to find the new me. Find who I was again. I needed to learn how to dream again.

This was a time for me to step out and try new things. It was a time to start saying yes to things that presented themselves to me. Even if I failed at them or decided I didn't like them, during this time, there was no pressure. I just got to sample things and figure out what I liked. Not because someone else told me I liked it or would be good at it. I went on multiple adventures.

After some time, I noticed myself gaining strength I never had before. The strength to set boundaries. I started seeing myself say no. I was saying no because I didn't want to do something instead of no because I was afraid of failing at it. This was foreign to me. But I started to see the things that didn't serve my true self, the person God developed me into. I saw the things that drained me versus energized me. My eyes were open to the things that came naturally to me and were fed by that internal spring versus the things that I was doing out of obligation, guilt, or fear of disappointing others. I even recognized things I did for fear of being rejected by others.

During this time of resting and having no pressure on me, I noticed certain things I naturally gravitated toward. I noticed the things I did in my free time, not because I had to but got to or wanted to. Initially, it was shocking because I became aware of just how many things in my life I had done because I didn't take the time to learn who I was. For example, a big part of my husband and my life was centered around hunting. We even ran a 501c3 that

Crystal Pain

was based around it. I started to see that I really didn't even like hunting. I was good at it, but I wasn't passionate about it. I did it to support him and spend time with Him. That's not a bad thing, but it was for me because I thought it was a part of my identity before. Turns out it isn't.

I enjoy hiking and being in nature, though. I enjoy working out and running. I enjoy fashion and interior design. I even love home improvement projects which I rarely participated in before. At this time, I wasn't working, but I saw that I was spending my time encouraging other friends who were opening businesses and had a great time helping them organize and set them up. I also got the opportunity to help a friend's daughter with her own job interview by getting her the perfect interview outfit in order.

All this may sound unimportant, but it isn't. It's critical to see the things you enjoy as well as the things that irritate you. Both will highlight areas you are gifted in or called to make a change in. They all point to the answers to the question, "Who Am I."

Many times in life, you will notice cycles. You might start to see a season where things come full circle, saying I've been here before. This feels like Déjà vu. I believe this is because God brings elements of healing to our lives, imparts wisdom, or sheds light on a subject. Things come back around and test us. They allow us opportunities to recognize where we took a wrong turn the first go around. They don't necessarily mean we have been called back into that area, but there is something that happened during the first encounter where we filed information incorrectly in our souls (mind, will, and emotions). He wants to point out these areas and give us a second chance at clarity and to "rearrange our filing system."

For me, this happened when I went back to school during this period in my life. I got my real estate license. I had obtained my license years ago when my daughter was a baby. This time I decid-

Crystal Pain of Re-Discovering Who You Are

ed to go back and get it because my father's last words to me were. "Baby, get your real estate license. You'll be good at it." So, I did this, thinking it must be God because Daddy said it before he died. I wanted to do what he wanted for me. I knew within the first week of this career I did not like it. It was just like the first time I had my license and reminded me of the college ad sales class. Something about it did not set well within me. I waited months before quitting, striving to face the fear. I didn't want to let it win. But then I realized I wasn't fighting the fear of rejection here. I was still living my life based on what someone else said for me to do. Now I know my daddy only wanted me happy and provided for, and he thought this might be something I was good at. I wasn't fighting a deep root inside myself; I wasn't fighting demons here. I was just going against something that didn't line up with my natural abilities and the assignment of God in my life. It wasn't something being fed by that natural spring of passion.

It's important to recognize what's behind the struggles, fears, and trials in your life. Is it a place in your life you need to set free from demonic attacks, or is it just a place God wants to bring refreshing to your soul and bring inner healing? If you revisit triggers in your life and speak God's truth over them, reminding yourself of everything He has already done for you in the past, He will do it again.

If you have encountered Satan's attack, it's going to be recognized by some key characteristics. One main thing is that it will cause torment. I think this is where we get most confused because when we are struggling, we automatically think the enemy is tormenting us. But if it truly is Satan, there are other things that will accompany this torment. Those two things will keep you from placing Christ in the position of your Savior, and they will keep you from serving Him effectively. If you aren't encountering these things in your struggle to find out "Who am I," just rest. Trust the process. You aren't required to pass every test right away. Take all the time you need and be led by the peace of God. Sometimes God just takes us back to areas for inner healing. They are just for a brief moment, not a life sentence. He won't let your giftings go to waste. It was his original design and desire to use you in the areas that He provides an unending supply of grace, peace, strength, and His comfort. Speak into those areas of God's Word. He will show Himself to you.

I was spending time one night in God's Word, and I knew he was telling me that I would be revisiting areas that I had been to before. He encouraged me by letting me know that I wasn't initially going to want to go there but that I needed to realize that just as I had changed, these areas would look different from my first experience in them. In the following weeks, I was invited to coffee with a women's writing group and to lunch with a beautiful woman who was trained in inner healing. My first reaction was, "God, I don't want to go, I've tried to write this book, but it's taken so many years already. And I will go to lunch, but I studied inner healing for ten years. I already know this area and how it works." I could hear Him again saying, "Just as you have changed, these areas will look different than your first experience."

(See Journal Entry "Edge of a Cliff" on page 259)

At this particular month in my life, I encountered real darkness and was very confused about my future. Still not wanting to go, that next Sunday at church, I was approached again by each one of these individuals. I agreed to both. After all, what do I have to lose? I chose to trust God, that this time they would look different.

God did not disappoint. Don't roll your eyes. I know I'm not the only one who doubts at times. These two opportunities for relationship changed the course of action in my life. Through the encounter with my gifted friend in inner healing, my eyes were opened to so much. She spent so many hours pouring into me fresh revelation on God's healing ways as well as reigniting a dormant

Crystal Pain of Re-Discovering Who You Are

passion inside me. Through this relationship, God began to download so much revelation to me regarding the recent attacks I had been in. Most importantly, I gained a mentor, a friend, and someone who would walk beside me in the kingdom.

The next meeting was the writing group. I left that group amazed at who was sitting around the table. There was someone representing a connection I had made from all areas of my life that stirred passions inside me. There were ladies representing the marketplace ministry, and ones called to steward the youth. There were also ladies who walked with great understanding regarding inner healing/ prophetic in life, as well as someone who had walked through similar attacks I had just walked through. There couldn't have been a more divinely orchestrated group. It was a Tribe of Women, my spirit so desperately hungered for. It was a pride filled with God's kingdom lionesses. We all were writing about similar things, eager to release God's Word and healing to the world around us.

God personally took me on a journey through my past. He took me all the way back to the very first time I was so desperately trying to figure out who and what I was to be in life. He let me revisit the college days and how I changed my major so many times. What I saw as a huge disappointment and a time of screwing up my life, He shed His light of truth on. I got to revisit some of the first areas I partnered with self-pity, and God showed me how He was beside me speaking the entire time.

He revealed to me that I initially chose nursing because He placed a hunger inside me to heal others of pain. Then He showed me that my want to be a mortician reflected the desire He put inside me to comfort those in times of struggle and grief. Then my changing my major again to advertising journalism was a direct reflection of the gift to pull out and advertise the strengths in others as well as writing. Retail was easy for me because He called me

Crystal Pain

to the marketplace. All these things are still there inside me. They never left. They took many different forms. They may even change forms again, but the heart in them, the passion that feeds them, will be a constant spring. It will be something when submitted to Him. He will always feed. Now I am aware of the contaminated lies Satan tried to sprinkle into the bread of life God has been baking for me my whole life.

CHAPTER 9

CRYSTAL PAIN OF ANIMALISTIC INSTINCT

Years ago, I was prompted to study the book of Proverbs daily. There are thirty-one chapters in Proverbs, which meant that if I studied one chapter a day, I would be able to read the book of Proverbs once a month. King Solomon is attributed with writing the book and was one of the wealthiest and wisest men to ever walk the earth. Great principles and ways to live life fill the pages. However, I love that even a prophet as wealthy and wise as Solomon included the wisdom of others within this book. He knew the importance of gleaning from others and sharing the spotlight.

Proverbs chapter thirty was written by a prophet by the name of Agur. I absolutely love this chapter and have gained so much insight reading it. Within this chapter, we can see that the prophet, Agur, describes himself as a beast and not a man. I could seriously relate to that statement. There are certain things that happen to you while walking through traumatic events that seem to place you in an animalistic survival mode. It's like you lose sight of reality and enter a state of just making it through the days. It's as if you are reaching for whatever you can find to fill the needs that your soul is aching for. Agur mentioned that he, too, was weary. He declared that he was someone who had yet to obtain human understanding

Crystal Pain

and linked it to the fact that he had yet to obtain the knowledge and understanding of God. Have you ever been here? So weary and turned around like you've been hit from so many different sides, you don't know which way is up. You start questioning your entire belief system.

Agur then describes God's works as flawless and our refuge. It's funny how even in those desperate times of confusion, there is a voice inside us that still holds on to God. There is something that is still pointing to Him as our safe haven. Deep down, we hunger to see how His ways are faultless and for Him to bring meaning to the horrible things we experienced. One thing that stood out to me about Agur is that in his desperate and weary cry, he asks only two things of God. First is for God to cleanse him of all lies and false beliefs. The second is that God gave him neither poverty nor riches, knowing that if he had too much, he might think he didn't need God, and if he had too little, he might steal from others and bring dishonor to God.

This request is so powerful! There is so much power in understanding that our confusion is rooted in lies and that for us to walk in clarity, we need to be stripped of everything we believe that does not line up with God's truths. It's also important that we realize that we do not know everything, and there is still so much of God's infinite knowledge we are to be gaining. There is something about humbly laying down our offenses in traumatic events, dying to our self-focus, and submitting to God even when we, in our carnal or animalistic mind, can't make sense of the situation. It's letting go of our pride and saying, nothing I do in my own strength can fix this, but you can. God, I still trust you. I still recognize you as the God of my life. You are my source.

The second part of this proverb is where I found most of my focus turning.

"Give me neither poverty nor riches but give me only my daily

Crystal Pain of Animalistic Instinct

bread. Otherwise, I may have too much and disown you and say, 'Who is the Lord?' Or I may become poor and steal, and so dishonor the name of my God" (Proverbs 30:8–9, NIV).

I noticed that most people interpret this passage automatically, referring to money. They relate it to the thoughts, "Don't give me too much money or possessions that I start to believe I don't need you. Or don't give me too little of these things where I become tempted to take them from others." It's strange how we so commonly associate God's goodness with his provision and blessing of materialistic things in our life. I do believe, however, that it goes even deeper than just money.

There is a TikTok influencer by the name of Topher. He uses TikTok as a platform to spread God's Word. He approaches random people and gives them an opportunity to answer three questions about the Bible. If they answer the questions, he offers to give them $100. Most people agree to play the game, but I recognized a pattern. Many, after getting the very first question wrong, automatically start opening up about their trials and traumas. Many discuss losing loved ones and how badly the last few years affected them. They would mention how they used to go to church, but after this loss, they became mad at God or started questioning Him. They'd say they haven't been back to church since.

Topher would give them the $100 even if they didn't get the questions correct as a way of showing God's mercy, grace, and love. These people would start crying at this tangible example of being blessed, even without perfection. You could see the lies break off them. I could see they were carrying a lie that God had punished them by taking their loved ones from them. There was a belief they had that God didn't want to bless them. I think they believed this because they thought if He did, then why did they have to go through so many bad situations? It was like a hardened part of their heart that caused them to reject God. I related to this.

That feeling of I served you, went to church, tried my best to be a good person, and you still didn't stop the trauma. So, why should I continue?

It was so awesome seeing that same part in them get a dose of the new revelation of God's love and grace. You could see the lies smashed into pieces the moment the money hit their hands. Topher would then share how he, too, had recently lost his mother and impart a truth that helped him in his walk. It was the fact that to be absent from the body was to be present with the Lord. That their loved ones were promoted to a life of pure joy, walking alongside Jesus now in heaven.

This was beautiful to watch. But it made me start thinking. Just as Agur mentions in Proverbs 30, it's important for us to see and recognize the lies we are believing and have God shake us free from them. Also, we need to recognize how much self-focus and our association with blessings and pleasure play a role in our relationship with God. It's necessary to make sure even this is placed under the management of God. If we place our life experiences only within a small diameter of our personal life and ignore the truth of God weaving together a much bigger picture, they can be like seeds that are planted inside our hearts that, if not plucked, outgrow into weeds of deception.

One of those things is a poverty mindset. This mindset can flow through both people with many blessings and possessions as well as those who walk in great lack. The poverty mindset tells us that there are only so many blessings to go around. We can believe that if someone else has something that we wanted, be that promotion at work or the newest car to hit the showroom floor, then we must have missed out on the opportunity. This gives way to covetousness and envy. We find ourselves unable to be happy about others' success and might even criticize them for having so much. I found myself stepping into this mindset right after a loss. It hit hard when I would see other friends or family members together, making memories with their husbands. On Father's Day, when people had their dads to spend the day with, I was jealous. I was unable to be happy for them because all I was aware of was my lack. I couldn't look past it. I couldn't imagine making memories again that were as special as the ones I made when they were alive.

On the other side of this, many have much but become stingy with it. Thinking if they give it away, there won't be enough for them in the long run. That they need to store it up just in case there is a possibility of a future dry season or that the blessings will stop. Both these views come from placing something other than God as the source. The truth is that God abundantly supplies all our needs. That's the trick there. It's according to our needs. But our needs turn quickly to wants if not submitted to Him. Yes, God wants to bless us and give us the desires of our hearts. He will even give these in abundance, but it requires our submission to Him. When not submitted to Him, we give way to jealousy, covetousness, envy, haughtiness, conceit, and greed.

(See Journal Entry "Pride in Lack, Warning Two" on page 252)

Proverbs 30 really focuses on greed. I want to take a moment to break this down. Greed may start out or look like desiring things, but it is very layered. It isn't just wanting material items but can grow into much more than that. It's wanting social status and obtaining influence, and the most dangerous is the desire for power. It's a tricky little way of twisting things around, taking our desires for things and flipping them around to allow self-control to take root in our heart. There is that little word we keep seeing throughout this book, you guessed it. Pride, the worship of self.

We are warned in this proverb of a generation that curses God and speaks evil of the church, one that sees themselves as pure and doing no wrong. That they would be filled with pride and see themselves as superior, looking down on others. Does this kind of

Crystal Pain

look like the world we live in today? I would say so.

I just want to show the sly little way Satan can try to get you to partner with this same mindset by using your trauma and hurt. By not submitting it under the rule and reign of God, allowing Him to speak the truth and heal into it, the wounds He could have used to bring forth wisdom can get distorted.

Maybe you do not recognize the egotistical, rebellious side of trauma. But can you see even a glimpse of becoming tethered (being tied so tight that you're no longer finding freedom) to self-focus? Something that says I deserve to be served. The "me, myself, and I" in a daily routine. Sure, when we think of a prideful person, we initially think of someone that thinks others should bow down to them and serve them because they are superior. But what about the person that says, "Bend toward me. I'm broken and deserve being served."

Let me stop here and reiterate that, yes, we should serve others. We should especially serve the widows and orphans, as God commanded. We should also be humble enough to ask for help and recognize the power in unity. However, what I am talking about is the manipulative accent someone might use, the one that goes with thinking you have a crown of merit, requiring others to bend toward you. It is one that wears a mask that is small and powerless yet employs this stature as a power to get others to do what they want.

I'm going to use a few of the items noted in Proverbs 30:16 and discuss ways I believe they can show up in our lives. I realize that many can safely say I have not struggled with any of these things. However, if you do happen to find any of them, strike accord, bring them before our loving Father God. Ask Him, "Is greed the source of this in my life?" If so, it only requires submitting it to Him and repenting. I think you'll feel a weight automatically lift off you as it breaks off your soul. Remember, this war is not

Crystal Pain of Animalistic Instinct

with flesh and blood but the things of darkness. Don't be tempted to beat yourself up and think you're pathetic. That is the shame of the enemy trying to keep you ensnared. This is a battle God is just waiting for permission to fight for us, we just submit to His healing power. You might start recognizing the patterns in the days to follow, but just stop and thank God that you are free from that thought process now. He will meet you there every time. Give Him time to rewire your brain. You've created neuropathways inside it and trigger responses. He can heal this, be patient with yourself and God's process. You didn't get there overnight; sometimes it takes time to get out of it. But His timing is perfect.

The first thing Agur associates with never being satisfied is "The Grave, yawning for another victim." I believe this is the spirit of death, and it sets out to first destroy your identity. It can come in when you measure your value and worth according to the world's views. By shifting your central focus of God and placing yourself at the center, you remove Him as your source. You then can start to define who you are by the praises of man. Gaining more and more status, or power, is how you feed and maintain these praises; this is a self-obtained identity. It can lead to developing character traits that ask for, demand, or require external reassurance. If these are never fed, your image begins to collapse. This could lead to depression, destructive behavior, or even self-harm. Ultimately making you "Graves Next Victim."

The second thing addressed is "The barren woman, ever wanting a child." I believe we all want to know that God can birth something out of our struggles. We find ourselves yearning to see the purpose in all we are going through, holding on to God's promise that all things work together for good. God desires to birth new things out of you. He wants to give you fresh revelation through your trials that will help equip others. Second Peter 1 tells us that God has given us all we need for a godly life through our knowledge of Him. He describes how gaining these qualities is a process

Crystal Pain

we must undergo. Don't allow your selfish desire to outweigh the perfect timing of God's process. We escape sinful desires by supplementing our faith with virtue, knowledge, self-control, steadfastness, godliness, brotherly affection, and love. If we are not willing to stay the course or grow impatient, you can terminate the development of these and find yourself stuck and unable to see past your pain. Increasing these qualities is what causes you to not remain in the barren land far longer than God ever intended.

The third thing mentioned is, "Thirsty soil, ever longing for rain." You might feel dry and empty, wanting to be filled up but can't find satisfaction. Something in you is having trouble receiving counsel, correction, or guidance from God or others. Greed can be found when you become focused on wanting more and more without thoroughly digesting what already is in front of you. A person ministering to you may have that more profound knowledge we seek, but we don't have the patience to hear them out. We might shut them out or interrupt them. We can place a wall up, preventing ourselves from truly listening to others' wisdom because we don't think they possess a grand enough word to stand up against what we have experienced. Maybe it's, "They don't understand me because they haven't walked through this," or "How could they possibly have the answer I am searching for without the experience to back it up." You also can get so focused on your pain and everything you lost; you shut God out. Possibly you turned to other things to gain guidance that are not rooted in God at the center. You find yourself seeking a quick fix. These sources might be placing the Self as the healer, manifester, or creator of your life. Without the power of God's love flowing, your soil has lost life-sustaining nutrients.

The fourth is "A raging fire, devouring its fuel." I believe this can come from thinking everything should bend toward you. You start taking everything from or using others for your own selfish gain without depositing anything else in return. You exclude

Crystal Pain of Animalistic Instinct

thankfulness and gratitude from the equation. You become like that raging fire, using others until they themselves are drained of supply and just moving on to the next.

Now, please know that there is an initial process of grieving that one must walk through. In this chapter, I am not referring to those stages of grief we all need to walk through. What I am addressing are those areas that we have found ourselves stuck in for years. I am referring to those areas that have gone on for so many years they have become torturously unbearable. They may have even felt like they created a domino effect, and we are spiraling out of control. You, with the guidance of the Holy Spirit, will recognize the difference between the two.

Satan's goal through trauma is to steal, kill, and destroy. It's the same goal that he uses always. The biggest weapon he uses is pride and the self-focus that comes from it. By getting us to take our eyes off the power of God and placing them on ourselves, he attempts to get us isolated and twists the truths. I'm so grateful that God has given us His Word to exchange those lies with truth, as well as the church and body of believers that will walk alongside us in community. We don't have to be perfect but just submit to Him.

CHAPTER 10

A TIME OF INTIMACY WITH HIM

I purchased a cute sign from a craft store near where I lived. As I was hanging it above my coffee bar, I noticed it was crooked. My first reaction was to pull it down and straighten it. But something inside me said, "Nope, I'm leaving it that way." The sign said Live in the Moment. I knew I wanted to start living by grace and not perfection. That sign was a daily reminder for me.

One day I was crying out to God. I sat in my room and told Him that I didn't even know what to pray. I just felt heavy. He said, "Then don't, just come and sit with me." I loved this invitation because, in the past, I had often thought that if I didn't have the perfect formula in my prayers that I wouldn't be effective in connecting with Him.

I turned off all the lights in my room. Then I turned on instrumental worship music, grabbed a pillow, and sat down on the floor. I just closed my eyes and focused on Jesus, giving the Holy Spirit full authority over my imagination. Within a few moments, the Holy Spirit took me on a journey through a vision. I saw Jesus there; He was reaching out His hand to me, walking along a beautiful beach. Such a peace came over me as I grabbed His hand

Crystal Pain

and looked into His eyes. We didn't exchange words at first. I just took in the glorious view that surrounded me. We sat down and just let the winds flow through our hair. Tears began to flow down my face. I remember thinking, *What's out there, God? What am I doing here? What's down the beach?* We didn't exchange words, but it was as if He could hear my thoughts.

He said, "Don't get ahead of me, dear one." Then He reached His hand toward my chest and ever so gently placed it over my heart. I knew He was saying I needed to allow Him to heal my broken heart first before anything, even before the intimate conversation took place. The warmth of His hand permeated my chest. I saw a vision of the inner workings of my heart, and there He was with a scalpel, scraping the arteries. There was a buildup that He removed first, and then a cleansing washing of water was run over it.

Then I was back on the beach with Him. I looked down at our feet and noticed He was wearing sandals, but my feet were barefoot. I asked why I didn't have sandals on like Him. He then told me that His thoughts for me outnumber the grains of sand, and He wanted me to feel the sand under my feet, to experience each thought. There was something so powerful about digging my feet in the sand and feeling each grain between my toes. I looked back up at Him, and He reached for my hand again and pulled me up. While standing there, I looked ahead of me and saw the unexplainably breathtaking sunset along the beach. I asked several questions without taking a breath. I asked Him, "What is ahead?" "Where does this beach lead?" "Are we going to walk in that direction?."

He laughed and said to me, "Don't concern yourself with what lies ahead. I will be bringing to you everything in this next season." Pondering the answer, I looked far out into the sea. There was a whale coming up for air, and I said, "Oh, look, Jesus!" He smiled and said, "Yes, those are my whales. They are called to the

A Time of Intimacy with Him

darkest depths of the sea. They are my missionaries, called to go out in the darkness and bring in those lost at sea. You have been trained in these ways, and I have given you many opportunities to experience and grow in them. But in this next season, I will be bringing to you everything."

No quicker than He finished His sentence, I saw a large fin swimming by. I said, "Oh gosh, is that a shark?" He said, "Yes, those are the counterfeits of the sea, swimming among the missionaries. They seek to devour and deceive everything in their paths. They are a danger to my people. But again, don't concern yourself with these things. Everything I have called you to, I will bring to you in this season." He continued, "I will bring many creatures of the sea to you, some will remain, and some will only stay for a moment."

He began to explain deeper as we explored the area of the beach we were standing in. He said, "See those? (There were crabs going across the beach.) Those creatures can lash out and pinch. It's their protective mechanism when they feel threatened. Many resort to violence, but I will always guide you in how to handle them."

We came across a jellyfish that had washed up on shore. I asked, "Is this dangerous, like the sharks"? He replied, "No, these are my beautiful creatures, but they can sting with their words when fearful. Like the crab, but they use words instead of actions. Again, I'll guide you."

Then there was a bunch of clams we saw. I said, "How do we get through those hard shells?" He laughed out loud, realizing that I was catching on. He said, "Don't rush them or try to pry them open. Lean into my guidance. You don't want to damage the process of them creating a beautiful pearl. They will open at the perfect time."

Walking around, I was just enjoying my time with Jesus. I felt so comfortable. We kept looking at the various creatures and all

Crystal Pain

the different tide pools. He was explaining how the tide pools are where the creatures that decide to stay will often be found. After a while of exploring, I asked Him what it was that my husband was doing. I said, "If you have called me to the beach, where is Nathan? I bet he is in a forest, hunting. He loves to hunt."

Jesus smiled, "Yes, he is hunting."

"Oh, my goodness!" I exclaimed. "I bet he is hunting bear. Is he hunting bear?"

Jesus told me, "No, he isn't hunting them, but he did tame one."

"Tame one?" I asked in disbelief. "Did he name it? I bet he named it!" I said with certainty.

Jesus was laughing again. We were having such a fun time. He assured me that "Yes, he named it."

I asked Him what he named it, and Jesus told me that he had called it "Frank." This made me giggle because only Nathan would give a bear a name like Frank. I then started wondering, *If Nathan isn't hunting bears, what is he hunting?* So, I asked Jesus.

Jesus looked me in the eyes, and I felt such a sense of significance in what He was about to say. He said, "He has been appointed to hunt the beasts that attack the boundary lines of the territories you are assigned to."

I started sobbing, and tears rushed down my face. Something about knowing that my husband and I were still working on the same project as a team. The things I feared most I didn't need to because he had already been appointed to destroy anything that was coming against my assignment to progress in the kingdom. I felt fear completely losing its grip.

Right after that, my dogs started barking at something outside my house, and I had to go. Jesus just said, "You can come back anytime. I'm always here."

A Time of Intimacy with Him

I was in awe at the intimate time Jesus allowed me. It just took me sitting at His feet, surrendering to Him, and He let me have this experience. He never got angry at all my questions or my impatience with wanting to look forward or look at the past. He walked with me through it all, gently answering each question and assuring me that He would guide me and not to concern myself with things outside of their timing or outside of the area He had designated for me. I also learned that asking the proper questions brought more answers than just firing out my emotions. Most of all, I learned to listen more than I spoke.

After this time with Him, I, in my spirit, felt refreshed. I knew what He was saying, but something inside me wanted more clarity. I absolutely love symbolism. I also know that God speaks through parables and symbolism throughout the Bible, so I began to dissect this experience I had. I started to take apart each symbol to see if I could clearly interpret it. I wanted more credibility. For years, God would speak to me in dreams, and being a seer in the spirit realm, I had studied many biblical symbol interpretation materials. So, I had a picnic on my bed. I grabbed these materials, my Bible and invited the Holy Spirit once more for guidance. I was ready for a feast of revelation. During this time of studying, I found several things to be true. I discovered even more depth to what Jesus was revealing to me. I think Jesus gives us dreams and visions and loves that draw us closer to Him in the dissection process. He says that He will reveal all mysteries to us.

Below are a few of the symbol interpretations taken from the book *A to Z Dream Symbol Dictionary* by Dr. Barbie L Breathitt. She is a recognized leader in dream interpretation, with healing, deliverance, signs, wonders, and miracles following.

A beach—is a calling to reach or touch the people of the world through evangelism or missions with the ebb and flow of Spirit.

A scalpel—symbolizes cutting away old, dysfunctional, or

Crystal Pain

diseased parts. It's seeking professional help from those who are skilled in the areas in which you need help. It can even be cutting off toxic, unhealthy relationships.

Sharks—ravenous appetites that represent lust and greed that selfishly devour whatever or whoever they want with no thought of anyone else but themselves. Worldly and sexual predators, judgmental spirit, rebellious, oppression, and attacks unexpectedly (Isaiah 27:1).

Bears—fighters who remove themselves from any further entanglements; they ignore issues through hibernation and isolation. Financial ruin, overwhelming competitiveness, economic loss (1 Samuel 17:34–36; 2 Samuel 7:8).

Boundary lines—limits to one's goals, restrictions on growth, or level of influence.

Territories—any area in which you are responsible for governing or representing. A sphere of interest or spiritual authority.

Tide pools—the homes of sea creatures. The inhabitants must be able to deal with frequent changes in order to survive or thrive. There is often exposure to predators such as bears or gulls at low tide.

Frank—means "Free to Be Yourself"

It was so cool to see that God was so gracious to bring me more confirmation in this study time. I especially loved that He showed me that the bear I had been fighting was now tamed and given a new name that allowed me truly to be "Free to Be Myself." It also gave me an awareness that the very things that God was bringing to me in this season would be fearful of this bear. That I could let them in on the secret that our Husband, God, has the power to tame it for them as well. There is nothing to fear while resting in the pools of His love.

I share all this to both encourage you and comfort you. I en-

A Time of Intimacy with Him

courage you to sit with Jesus and let Him pour into your vision. I also hope that you recognize the areas in your life that need to be submitted to God's healing love. I want you to see that He is gently walking beside you. He is working everything together for your next chapter. He is patient and so kind, even when we are impatient and full of worry. By locking eyes with Him and keeping Him at the center of everything, you will walk in overwhelming peace. There is an enemy that sees you as weak and is trying to get you off track, trying to distort the truth. However, God desires more than anything to partner with you in battle. Where you are weak, He is strong. He will bring alongside you a tribe, a community of believers, to help. Walk the process and give yourself permission to make mistakes. God doesn't require perfection. He wants only for us to yoke up with Him. He wants to make the burden light. He also wants to bring wisdom to the wounds and to use you to help grow and develop a stronger generation. He desires for you to be free of all lies that have tried to attach themselves to you and for you to step into the person He created you to be. He wants you to be "Free to Be Yourself"! Trust Him. Lean in and sit at His feet when you feel weary. He's got you! The future looks bright for you.

(See Journal Entry "Essential Breeding Hens" on page 220)

CHAPTER 11

CRYSTAL PAIN OF NEW BIRTH

I've mentioned that there can be barriers in our souls that prevent us from receiving the blessings of God. If these go unattended for too long, they can show up in our bodies as illnesses. God is often standing there with all you have prayed for, but you're unable to receive it. You must make room for His blessings and rid yourself of things taking up this space. You also must be able to see them through His eyes. We are made up of three parts: body, soul, and spirit. God desires for us to be whole in all three of these areas.

"Now may the God of peace make you holy in every way and may your whole spirit and soul and body be kept blameless until our Lord Jesus Christ comes again" (1 Thessalonians 5:23, NLT).

Throughout this book, I have given many examples of ways the enemy disrupted my spirit and soul from being at peace. I discussed the many battles I faced because of the lies I came back into agreement with or the spiritual attacks that I was voluntarily allowing in my life. The moment we accept Jesus Christ as our Lord and Savior, we are born again and made new.

"Therefore, if anyone is in Christ, the new creation has come. The old has gone, the new is here" (1 Corinthians 5:17, National Living Translation).

Crystal Pain

We are no longer responsible for bearing the weight that sin places on us. Those things that once controlled us, through Him, we are given authority over. This doesn't mean that the temptation to sin stops advancing toward us or the enemy stops trying to influence our thoughts. It is our responsibility to take up our cross daily. This means that we must recognize these things and remind them that they are a part of our old man. We are to remind ourselves that they have been nailed to the cross with Jesus and submit them to God. They have no power or right to inflict us. They can only come in through the doors we voluntarily open to them.

Just for clarification—it is our spirit that we invite Jesus to come and reside inside. The moment we accept Him, our spirit is made clean. We are considered righteous and holy through Him.

Our soul, conversely, consists of our mind, will, and emotions. This part of us is biblically referred to as our flesh. It is our thoughts, our desires, and our emotional feelings (sometimes reactions). This part of us we are instructed to offer as a living sacrifice to God. It is the "dying to the flesh" that we often talk about. We must make sure that we take each thought captive, and in doing this, we will be able to discern God's will in our lives.

"Do not be conformed to this world, but be transformed by the renewal of your mind, that by testing you may discern what is the will of God, what is good and acceptable and perfect" (Romans 12:2, ESV).

Since Jesus resides in our hearts, Satan cannot touch us there. However, this does not stop him from trying to influence our soul. He tries to contaminate our thoughts, hijack our desires, and negatively influence our emotions. In doing this, we can often see the effects of such wrong thoughts, uncontrolled emotions, and pursuit of wrong motives show up in our body. Throughout scripture, we can see examples of how the soul affects our bodies and that the two are closely linked. Proverbs explains that one whose heart is crushed struggles with sickness. God desires for us to prosper, though. He desires that our soul prosper and that we be in good health.

"Beloved friend, I pray that you are prospering in every way and that you continually enjoy good health, just as your soul is prospering" (3 John 1:2, TPT).

As I was on this healing from trauma journey, there was a clear sequence I could see. God was realigning all the areas within my soul back under His perfect will in my life. He was showing me the areas that I needed to renew my mind, resubmit my desires, and lay down my selfish ambitions in life. Even though there were times I felt like I was going from one battlefield to the next, each time, there was more freedom won. There were many layers to penetrate my soul. With each battle and each layer being pulled back, I would encounter a new level of His peace. I was blessed to experience just how much He desires to bring us wholeness in body, soul, and spirit.

About a year after this traumatic journey started in my life, I started to struggle with an irregular menstrual cycle. Sometimes I would skip my cycle for two months at a time. I understand this can be an uncomfortable topic to discuss, but I believe there was a valuable truth God revealed to me in my struggle. By this time, I lost a lot of weight; however, I started noticing that my stomach was starting to distend. I would compare this increase in size to that of a woman who was around three months pregnant. One day, while at work, I had a sharp pain in my abdomen that knocked me to the ground. It absolutely took my breath away. I went to the emergency room. After several hours, blood tests, and a CT scan, they determined that a cyst had developed on my ovary. They informed me that it had ruptured, and this was causing the pain.

In the years following, this became a frequent occurrence for me. Once, I had three cysts developing at one time on my ovaries.

Crystal Pain

They always seemed to go away on their own, but the symptoms that I experienced during the waiting time were so uncomfortable. Eating the smallest amount of food would cause me to quickly feel extremely full. My digestion would be hindered, and my emotions would become out of control. Each time, I looked pregnant and was embarrassed because I was in my mid-forties. I was paranoid about what people would think.

I made several visits to various OB-GYNs, and they all told me that it was something I would just have to deal with. There wasn't much they could do. One offered to place me on birth control pills to try and regulate my hormones, but that was about all they suggested. I was not satisfied with this answer. I'm a child of God, and He is a God of healing and miracles.

I began to pray about this and ask the Lord what the spiritual root of this issue was. I went back to the understanding I had gained regarding us being made up of three parts. I grabbed ahold of the truth of God's Word that told me that I was to prosper in health as my soul prospered. I would not entertain the opinion that this prognosis is something I was going to have to deal with for the rest of my life. I needed the Holy Spirit to help me discern where in my soul I needed to be transformed. What was I holding on to that was preventing me from making room to carry His prosperity and health. Was there yet another lie I believed that needed to be submitted back under His truth? I remember Romans 12:2 tells us, "That by testing you may discern what is the will of God." I knew His promise but was lacking discernment. This lack of discernment was keeping me in bondage to this illness. I was determined not to have to "manage" any ill health but wanted to learn the prevention of it. So, I asked the Lord. If my body was in bondage, where in my soul was I still in bondage? What part of my thoughts, desires, and emotions were still not in alignment with your truth?

God first walked me through what an ovarian cyst actually was

Crystal Pain of New Birth

and the effects they have on the body. Women create eggs that develop and mature in the ovaries, and each month, they are released. Inside the ovary, there is a sac that breaks open and releases the egg. Without giving a full science lesson, I will just inform you that basically, the formation of ovarian cysts stops the egg from being released properly. It can either prevent it altogether or it interrupts the natural process of development.

It was becoming clear to me. Something in my soul was preventing the new development that God wanted to do in and through me. My body (ovaries) was not functioning properly and blocking my ability to release eggs, just as my soul was not functioning properly and blocking my ability to release seeds for the kingdom. I realized that I was still not seeing myself as worthy or even capable. Part of me was not allowing the seeds of wisdom God had developed inside my spirit to travel deep down inside my heart and attach to my womb. The two were related. Once I allowed God to reveal and unblock these things in my soul, I knew my body would follow suit.

Please understand that I am not insinuating that what God revealed to me as the spiritual root of my cysts is also the root cause for everyone dealing with ovarian cysts. I can only speak for what He revealed in my soul that needed realignment. I do, however, believe that He can show others various blocks to lead them on a path to receiving healing too.

What was it? What was delaying my ability to release these seeds of wisdom?

I was drawn to the story in 2 Kings 4 of Elisha and the woman from Shunem. In this story, the woman and her husband allowed Elisha to stay in their home when he was passing through their town. Because of her kindness, Elisha asked how he could bless her. She was already wealthy and had the most material things you could need. She didn't have a son, though. Elisha spoke over her that she would bear a child. The woman's first response was, NO! She said, "Don't deceive me and get my hopes up." As this story proceeds, the woman does give birth to a son. But while he is still young, he dies. After his death, the Shunammite woman travels by donkey to find Elisha. When she is met by him, she falls at his feet and again mentions, "I told you not to deceive me and get my hopes up." In the end, Elisha goes back to Shunem with her, and the boy is healed. Can you find the part that stood out to me?

"Don't get my hopes up," she said. I could feel the woman's fear in this story. That fear was familiar. It makes you hesitant to grab hold of hope for a better future. It is one that is accompanied by disappointment. I, myself, have had a fear of not wanting to get my hopes up. This fear had caused many other symptoms in my life. God revealed that it was a huge barrier in my soul. It was hindering my ability to digest the words of prosperity God was speaking over me. It affected my emotions, and I developed anxiety around the thoughts of not being good enough. I cried that I couldn't handle the pressure and became overwhelmed. It was inhibiting me from releasing the seeds inside me to birth something new.

I feared starting something new while in my mid-forties. How could I start all over at my age? Life with my husband was filled with seeing dreams we had carried for years come to fruition. That process was accompanied by a lot of pain. I understood the strength and energy that goes into birthing a dream. There were so many mistakes, obstacles, and wrong turns along the journey. I didn't know if it was in me to start again. Especially if this one ended in disappointment like I had the first season. Having the dream end, with losing my partner and best friend, is something I don't want to face again.

I was seeing the comparison between body and soul again. I recognized the correlation between it affecting my ability to con-

Crystal Pain of New Birth

sume His words spoken over me and my emotions being unregulated. There was a similarity in the way cysts caused me to not be able to consume food and caused emotional irregularities. How did I get over this fear? God's perfect love casts out all fear, and that love often comes to us in and through others. It did for me, anyway.

Over coffee with a few friends, I broke down while discussing how hard it was for me to dream again due to the fear of disappointment I carried. One of them shared with me an analogy about disappointment. She said to think of it as two parts: the dis- and the appointment. Dis means to remove. When you see the meaning, you realize that disappointment was actually the removal of an appointment. When my husband passed away, that assignment or appointment had been fulfilled. It was a blessing that I was allowed the opportunity to play a starring role in such a beautiful story. It was time for me to have another appointment, to receive another assignment, and to play a starring role in another story. It was the closing of one book and the beginning of an entirely different one. I could not let the fear of the pain in my first story stop me from birthing a new one. Even though I was starting a new book, I was playing the same character. My traits had just gone through some development.

God reminded me of a few positive changes in my character since the loss of my husband. I made a lot of mistakes, but in the end, I was greatly humbled. That is a great foundation for a new build. I also began to know my value outside of works or the praises of man. I now understand the importance of community and listening more than I speak. These are also great tools that will help me in the construction of a new dream. He had been using everything to equip me the entire time. This type of change, His change, isn't temporal. His change is in your framework. One board is out of place, and you've become awakened (through your previous round) to recognize and fix issues more quickly. This will

Crystal Pain

help you prevent future more aggressive pains that could lie ahead. He always changes us in a way that equips us to advance with ease and reliance on Him. The first round did hurt. My flesh was dying, and my foundation wasn't concrete. However, change, His change, doesn't always come cheap. But once you obtain it, it never loses its value. That value is accompanied by great strength.

Now I understood that I was equipped and capable of birthing something new. I saw that I could be used again to share the good news of Jesus. But I was still sensing something out of line that was stopping me from moving forward. There was still another layer. There was a removal that needed to take place. Sometimes when you develop cysts on your ovaries, they go away on their own, and other times they require surgery to remove them.

God was still there, and He was still guiding me. He is, The Great Physician. He is there to thoroughly see the surgery through to completion. I have mentioned the backsliding that I was a part of throughout my grief journey. The partnership with things from my past involved drug use, alcohol, relationships, lifestyles, and beliefs that did not line up with God's best for me. These things had become places where I had placed myself and my desires over those of God's. They were areas that I chose to fulfill my flesh, give way to greed, and partner with demonic forces. Whether they were done through confusion and an attack of the enemy or through disobedience didn't matter. I knew that I had been in active idolatry. I had repented and knew God had forgiven me, but I was walking around with such a heaviness. How could I have lived a life sold out to the Lord, been used by Him for years, and still committed adultery on Him? I was having such a hard time forgiving myself for these things. I was having a hard time metabolizing this shame.

I was in a counseling appointment with one of my pastors with his DMCC (Doctorate in Christian Counseling), Dr. Terry Brown. He is someone whom I hold with much esteem. During this ses-

Crystal Pain of New Birth

sion, he walked me through a visual that totally changed me. He informed me that my armor was covered in black and wanted me to envision him pulling back the darkness like a curtain with both his hands and peeking through at me. He physically held his hands up as if he was holding curtains back. Then he looked at me and said, "I see you, and welcome back." I burst into tears. He then went on to say, "When you feel strong enough and ready, I will turn them over to you to hold open." After some time, he looked at me, still holding them, and said, "Are you ready?" Without speaking, I nodded yes. I then grabbed the two sides and held them open. I was still crying. I was locking eyes with Him while holding them open. I recognized that he had seen me. He saw me through God's eyes, and he had a kindness of approval in his eyes.

Then, my pastor (Dr. Brown) asked me, "Now, what are you going to do with them?" After a moment of hesitation, I took my two fists (holding them open) and motioned my hands to the air. I handed them over to God and then released my grip. Physically I felt the weight and burden of shame breaking off me. Encountering, in that moment, the fullness of Jesus carrying all our sins on the cross and how He washes us clean. I felt His forgiveness and was then able to forgive myself.

In the weeks to follow, when I would feel shame try and attach itself to me, I would walk through this technique over and over. Pulling away the darkness and turning it back over to God. I felt this was another level of freedom I was now walking into. It was the scales falling off my eyes and something that allowed me to see, with clarity, God moving in my life again. Now I was able to seek Him deeper and allow Him to take me on a journey that, before, I might not have received. We were going to visit a place deep within my history.

CHAPTER 12

CRYSTAL PAIN THROUGH THE GENERATIONS

The Bible is filled with symbolism. I've found this to be an aspect that intrigues me and one of the reasons why I love studying it. It's constantly speaking to you on deeper levels. You can read it, and the Holy Spirit will highlight a word for you. After studying that specific word in-depth, you often start seeing a whole new level of what the Lord was telling you in that scripture, chapter, or even a person. It's interesting how we can walk through life in a similar way. We have a choice in how we perceive it. Often, we choose to only view it on a surface level, filtering it through only what we can observe by our own carnal senses. We are so limited to the information that is at hand, yet we are quick to make assumptions based on that limited knowledge regarding situations. We may judge others on appearance, their actions, and words they spoke out of context. Rarely do we stop to hear, inquire, or gain information that paints the full picture. It's like gazing at the moon and failing to see the magnitude of galaxies that surround it and how truly small our viewpoint is. It's astonishing how God keeps everything in perfect order, yet we fail to see all He is doing at once.

Symbolism revolving around a person's name is something

129

Crystal Pain

that truly grabs my attention. I find it so interesting that throughout the scriptures, we see that the name given to a baby turns out to be reflected in their purpose, physical traits, or even personality traits. For example, look at Jacob and Esau. The name Esau means "hairy," and this was a physical trait he possessed. On the other hand, Jacob means "deceiver." We know that he deceived his father to gain the blessing originally intended for Esau. This name reflected a personality trait he possessed. I love how God often changed a person's name to denote a new identity or calling on their lives. How powerful it would be to have God Himself change the trajectory of your life by speaking a new identity over you. Simon was changed to Peter, Jacob was changed to Israel, and Saul was changed to Paul. I truly believe there is so much power in a name. Jesus's own name means "Deliverer" or "Savior."

The Lord tells us in His Word that our words carry so much power and authority. They have the power to create life or death.

"The tongue has the power of life and death, and those who love it will eat its fruit" (Proverbs 18:21, NIV).

This realization makes me stop and truly think about the words that come out of my mouth. Am I speaking life or death over myself? James 3 warns us about the power of a tongue. He compares it to the small rudder that steers an entire ship, a bit in a horse's mouth that can control its movement, and even a small spark that sets a forest completely on fire. It tells us that the tongue can set the whole course of one's life.

While reflecting on these two insights, I began to wonder about my own name. I questioned its origin, its meaning, and the history behind it. I also wondered if there was anything attached to it that I had been speaking over my life that didn't necessarily need to be spoken. I wanted everything that I was aligning myself with to be dedicated to the Lord and washed with His cleansing blood. If anything wasn't connected to the purpose, identity, and call God

Crystal Pain through the Generations

had for my life, I wanted to know. I wanted everything under the authority of God and to be speaking only life into my future.

While researching my name, God took me on a discovery that was very eye-opening. He showed me things that had become HUGE in hindering my ability to step forth into complete wholeness and health. These specific areas led to revealing negative things that had been attached to my entire bloodline. This hindrance had tried to take up residency in my family line and inflicted misguidance for generations. God had already created an exit plan, and my mother was the first in my family to have her eyes opened to see part of that plan.

My mother had named me after her stepmother. I wondered why she chose her stepmother and not my biological grandmother. After my grandparents divorced, my grandfather remarried, and my mom (along with her siblings) went to live with them. My mom's stepmother was a working mom, and she was very structured. I remember Mom telling me stories about all the chores she was responsible for while growing up. She was expected to have dinner on the table every night by 5:00 p.m. and all the laundry and ironing done each week. Why would my mom name me after a woman that was so strict and structured? Why would she want me to carry the name of someone that wasn't even in our blood? I kept these questions in the back of my mind as I continued to research.

I asked my mom often about my biological grandmother. When she described her, it was obvious to see that she and my mom's stepmother were quite different. You could say they were even the opposite of each other. The way I heard the story was while living with my biological grandmother, my mom was allowed to do many things. My grandmother was more like a friend to them. Mom told me that once, at the age of fifteen, Grandma even let her smoke around her. My mom didn't have very many rules at all when she was allowed to stay with my grandmother.

Crystal Pain

Before you develop any wrong ideas about the parenting skills of my grandma, please let me explain a little about her upbringing. My biological grandmother was given up as a child, and she and her siblings were raised in an orphanage. My grandmother was not raised under the constant love of parents, nor did she have an example of what a normal household should look like. She didn't understand the value of structure or discipline in a child's life. When she had children of her own, she was left to develop these skills by herself. My grandma did the best she could. I can only imagine that she wanted nothing more than to have a house filled with a family where everyone was happy. I imagine that she spent her whole life trying to be the best she could, fighting this "orphan title" that whispered inside her the entire time. I'm sure it told her she would never be good enough. It was saying if she wasn't nice, things would be taken from her or wanted to leave her. It whispered that she was different and didn't really fit.

My mother, on the other hand, had not been raised in church. She didn't have anyone introduce her to Jesus until later in life. She wasn't aware of the scriptures telling you to train up a child in the way they should go or any biblical principles regarding family. But God still gave her an awareness that she was able to discern the difference between these two parenting skills. There was still a check inside her spirit that made her able to discern that something regarding my biological grandmother's behaviors was not something she wanted to be passed down to her daughter. I don't believe she realized it, but there was an unconscious decision she was making. But when she named me, she gave me the name of her stepmother. At that moment, I believe in the spirit realm, a declaration was made that shifted our generational line. I just wasn't aware of its magnitude until later in life.

In Exodus 34, we see that there is a curse that bestows punishment on children for the sins of their parents. We see that this punishment for their sins goes to the third and fourth generations.

Crystal Pain through the Generations

"Yet he does not leave the guilty unpunished; he punishes the children and their children for the sin of the parents to the third and fourth generation" (Exodus 34:7, NIV).

This is Old Testament law, and today we know that we are set free by the blood of Jesus at the cross. When we come before the Father in repentance, this curse is broken. He makes us a new creation, and we live in complete freedom. However, it is our job to recognize these curses and allow Jesus access to them. I do not believe that when the Word of God refers to a curse in this scripture that it is talking about a curse in the way we understand it today. Rather it refers to the mindsets that are developed in sinful ways and those thought processes that are passed down from generation to generation. It is easy to be confused as to why we might be struggling with something. We might search ourselves and not be able to make sense of why a specific area in our lives is difficult for us to overcome. Sometimes these areas are not a direct reflection of something you yourself did, but it is something that has been passed down through your biological line. It's a distorted truth or lies in the way you process information, which causes your pain or discomfort. Maybe this is depression, anxiety, feeling unworthy, etc.

There is a popular quote from Stephi Wagner, MSW and Executive Director, Founder, and Lead Educator of the Mother Wound Project. She says, "Pain travels through families until someone is ready to feel it."

Mark Wolynn is the director of the Family Constellation Institute and the author of the book *It Didn't Start with You*. In his book, he explains how the traumas of our parents, grandparents, and even great-grandparents can live in our unexplained depression, anxiety, fears, phobias, obsessive thoughts, and physical symptoms. He explains how scientists are now calling this "secondary PTSD."

Crystal Pain

Wolynn says,

> *Just as we inherit our eye color and blood type, we also inherit the residue from traumatic events that have taken place in our family. While our physical traits are easily discernible, this emotional legacy is often hidden from us. Anxiety, fear, financial worries, depression, illness, and unhappy relationships can all be forms of our unconscious inheritance. Unresolved traumas, some going back two or three generations, can ensnare us in feelings and situations that don't even belong to us. They can forge a blueprint for our lives and can even pass it on to our children. It doesn't have to continue. Inherited family trauma can end.*

I used these examples to show how patterns of generational dysfunction are seen in the psychology world as well as the theological world. Patterns of dysfunctional pain and mental and emotional wounds have been discovered by many to go back for generations within family structure. People have been trying to bring reason to the why for decades. One unknown author, coming from a viewpoint of the New Age Movement, even stated, "Somewhere along the line, a child will be born whose charge is to feel it all. These are your shamans, priest and priestesses, your healers. You call them mental health patients and label their power as depression, anxiety, bipolar disorder, and the like. But these are the ones who are born with the gift of feeling."

As a person who stands on the teachings of God's Word, I do not agree with everything within secular teaching. I feel the importance of reinstating something that I discussed earlier. We cannot remove God from being our source. He is the one who reveals all mysteries. He is the one that is speaking to us and guiding us. It is His power that lives in us and flows through us. I do not agree

Crystal Pain through the Generations

with shamanism or New Age healing practices. I believe that these are distortions of God's truth and remove Him as the source. I do, however, know that we can hear God's voice and that His healing flows through us as believers. I also know that many believers tangibly feel the presence of God. In Romans 12, as well as 1 Corinthians 12, you read about the gifts of the Holy Spirit and how they operate in various members of the body of Christ. We see how they play a role in building up the church and connecting them to each other in wholeness.

Many of my friends are intercessors and spend hours in prayer for our country and others. Many of my acquaintances have sensed shifts in the atmospheres, felt physical pains of others, and even discerned things around them through the five human senses. Be that through touch, smell, taste, hearing, or seeing into the spirit realm. They have submitted their entire physical body to the Holy Spirit to use for His glory. They use their specific giftings for the building up and encouragement of others. I find it interesting that science and psychology back up the Word of God, and the parallels in teachings are undeniable. I believe that we need to be a generation that rises and declares wholeness for not only our families but the entire body of Christ. It's time we stand up and say. It ends here! Pick me, God, charge me! I will stand in the gap.

"Then I heard the voice of the Lord saying, "'whom shall I send? And who will go for us?' And I said, 'Here am I. Send me!'" (Isaiah 6:8, NIV)

These malformed areas in our generational line need to be placed under God. These are the areas that affect our bodies as well. Once we come to a place of wholeness in our mind and emotions, our body will follow. I have even found in scripture examples of curses flowing through generational lines until one of the descendants stood up and put a stop to it. We can see this in Abraham's story. Even he, being the father of faith, had a curse that

Crystal Pain

flowed through his family, and it was easily seen operating through his offspring. By studying his story, you see he was a liar. He lied about Sarah being his wife out of fear of man. His son, Isaac, was a liar too. He actually told the exact same lie as his father and lied about Rebeka being his wife. Isaac's son, Jacob (even named deceiver), was, you guessed it, a liar. Finally, there came a child, Joseph, who rose up and put a stop to it. It wasn't an easy road for Joseph, and he withstood many trials and rejections, as well as being misunderstood. But nonetheless, he persevered. He was used to changing the trajectory of his entire family line.

I shared that I was a very rebellious young adult, and my parents had raised us in a strict religious atmosphere. But as I got older, both my parents and I recognized the difference in religion verses being in relationship with Christ. We were eventually plugged into a life-giving church and found ourselves under the covering of a pastor who taught us truth. In this season, my mother and I grew to become very close. We were able to be open about our history and share everything with each other. During this time, she had discovered some news that was disturbing about her parents and an area she had to walk through for forgiveness and her own inner healing.

She was informed that when her parents first found out they were pregnant with her, they attempted to abort her. This attempt obviously did not work, thank the Lord. But this information jolted a revelation inside me. I saw a correlation in the family pattern. My great-grandparents rejected my grandmother and placed her in an orphanage as a child, and my grandparents initially rejected my mother by trying to abort her. I revealed to my mother a secret I was holding: I had rejected my first pregnancy and successfully had an abortion when I was in college. I recognized the patterns that my grandmother, mother, and I delt with. There was an active evil within our family line trying to stop or hinder it from reproducing strong offspring. It was an attack on not only us seeing our value but others seeing the value we had in life.

136

Crystal Pain through the Generations

On top of this, I recognized character traits we collectively dealt with. We battled with a sense of abandonment, loneliness, alienation, and isolation. Even in a crowd, sometimes I could remember not feeling like I fit in. I went to great lengths to just be liked and loved by all, even if this meant not being true to who I was. I did anything just to "fit." The fear of not being accepted controlled me. That fear even went as far as me not stepping into a call God placed on my life for fear of being rejected or made fun of. This even transferred to my own parenting beliefs. I believed that I wasn't good enough to be a mom and that I would mess up raising my own daughter. I thought I would guide her wrong and cause her to walk a difficult road. I definitely believed I didn't deserve to be a mother, especially after what I did to my first child.

There was also something in me that thought I had to earn God's love. These thoughts were all related to that orphan mindset that was transferring down our generational line. It would for years whisper that God didn't really want me, but if I did what He asked, I would be useful enough for Him to keep. I know, as a Christian who is well-versed in the scriptures, that this doesn't make sense. These are all lies. But our battle was not with flesh and blood here. It was a principality of darkness that God tells us He overcame at the cross. When we invite Jesus into our hearts, the power and authority over these principalities reside in us, too.

This is where I recognized that there was a deeper root to all this. There was a generational curse that I was still partnering with. This curse had been broken off me, but I was still allowing it to control me. I am not saying that I was ever possessed by a spirit here, but these mindsets can oppress us. These mindsets will try and control you. I, like many others, was determined to be the generation that stood up and said, I see you! Your lies must bow, and I will not partner with them any longer. You are nailed at the cross with Jesus and have no right to torment me or any of my future offspring. The curse ends with me!

Crystal Pain

"Like a fluttering sparrow or a darting swallow, an undeserved curse does not come to rest" (Proverbs 26:2, NIV).

I had several good years of walking in the freedom of this. Then after the trauma of losing my husband, it circled back around trying to regain access to my life. It found me in a raw state of feeling abandoned, lonely, forsaken, and isolated by the pandemic. This attack came in that moment of weakness.

God gave me the keys to break free at the cross, so it was my job to use them. It is as simple as putting them in the door and locking them shut. I stood in the gap and asked God to forgive my family and myself for the agreement we came into with this orphan mindset. I thanked Him for His Spirit of Sonship that would now rule and reign over our lives again. Just like I did with shame, I pulled back the black curtain covering my eyes and heard God say, "I see you." I turned over the reins to God. And He took them!

I love how God worked on my mother and allowed her this wisdom. God was using her before I was even born. He even used her before she even realized the magnitude of what she truly was battling. He used her in this war against the orphan mindset even before she herself saw with clarity that it was operating in our family. She just knew that she wanted a better life for her descendants.

This generational curse was destined to lose its power in our family. Like Joseph, I was the fourth generation, and I was willing to stand up and say it ends with me! My daughter will not struggle with these curses. She will walk a life of freedom. She will know the Lord as her Savior and friend. She will know her true identity outside of a family name. Going forward, she will find her identity in the name of Christ. We carried a new name on our family line. We were not orphans; we didn't come from broken families. We were part of a kingdom of God, given rule and reign. We were Children of the Most High! We were a part of God's family. God had a starring role for us to play, and nothing was going to stop

Crystal Pain through the Generations

God from birthing new life out of us.

Now, I want to return to the second part of this story. My mother named me after my stepmother. Remember how God was showing me that our words have power and that what we speak over our lives can bring life or death? He tells us that they are powerful enough to change the entire direction of our life. I wanted to break anything tied to what I had been calling myself. God revealed the generational curse attached to my mother's side, and we broke any agreement to that. But I still needed to dive deeper into the name I had actually been calling myself.

(See Journal Entry "Don't Be a Puppet" on page 244)

My step-grandmother's name was Charlene. It means "little woman" as well as "free spirit." I always found this funny because I am not even five feet tall in stature, and my mother always used to refer to me as her free-spirited child. Let's face it. I was a bit of a wild child. I often called myself the black sheep. These were easy things to renounce once I gave my life to Christ. But what I found interesting was regarding the death of my step-grandmother. I asked my mom how she passed away. She informed me that she suffered from reoccurring cysts and eventually developed ovarian cancer. She lost the battle with this cancer, and that is how she passed.

There it was! There was the exact struggle I had been in for years and a fear I was harboring regarding the prognosis given to me. I believe my step-grandmother had some amazing qualities. There were qualities that I found in common with her and found honorable. She was a businesswoman, she kept an orderly home, she was fashionable, and she loved her husband well. But I was not going to speak over my life the curses attached to her name. I renounced this the moment I recognized them. I sanctified my name and dedicated it to Jesus for His cleansing, and through the power He gave us, I rebuked anything on that name that did not line up with His will in my life. I still go by the name Cecily Charlene, but I believe at that moment, God added to it His blessing. He can and will do this for anyone.

Let's say that in your previous story you played the role of a telephone. I know this sounds corny, but bear with me. Let's say you were a rotary phone. You had an amazing role. You connected people to each other, allowed communication between them, and even closed the distance gaps. Of course, you could only be used in certain areas or at certain times. But you accomplished a great task.

In this next season, God is still going to use you as a phone. But He is going to add to your gifts and talents. He is evolving you and will give you a changed name. You will still go by the name of a phone, but He calls you a "cell" phone now. You will still be connecting with people, but there will be a clearer connection. This time, there will be picture references that increase your memories and facts that are available right at your fingertips. You can even be used everywhere you go and at any time you want. Your ability to communicate will greatly increase. When you don't have the right words, you will be able to use pictures and can send a letter in the blink of an eye when unable to speak. Don't worry about boundaries, either. You will be able to set these too. You will be able to choose who you want to talk to or even block out nuisances. It could take you some time to learn how to operate this new way, and it could be difficult at times. You won't be forced to change, though. The choice is yours.

My name, Cecily Charlene, actually means "Free Spirited Little Woman of Blind Faith." Blind faith can sound kind of scary. But God says that we are to walk by faith and not by sight. That choice remains in my hands. I am ready to say yes to God again. Ready to not allow anything that is stopping or interrupting the release of fresh seeds to be birthed in and through my life. I am

Crystal Pain through the Generations

small in stature but not in might, and my spirit is under the rule of the Lord, no longer free to serve my selfish desires, my pains, and discomforts. I allow God's wisdom to take root in my life.

I pray that by reading my story and the many roads God allowed me to travel down in my journey, you are able to see and absorb that wisdom for yourself. I know that no two stories are the same, just as no two people are the same. We are all unique, and the world around us needs to hear from you as well. Our daddy God desires us all to walk in freedom, to be empowered by His love, and to spread the good news. The testimony of Jesus in our lives is the Spirit of prophecy.

"For it is the Spirit of prophecy who bears testimony to Jesus" (Revelations 19:10, NIV).

This means that telling your story, it holds such power that it brings freedom to others. He desires to bring the same freedom that was deposited in one life to all His children's lives. I believe that He is preparing a great church in this hour. The enemy has tried hard to stop that preparation. I pray that you hold on tight, never give up, and see that His ways are so much greater than we in our carnal minds can grasp. Take time with Him. Sit at His feet. Let Him complete that work for you. Allow yourself to become a new creation in Him. You are created with purpose and on purpose.

He wants you to use your story. He is giving you a platform through your journey that allows you to greatly communicate with credibility. Your story is a picture that speaks, one that carries memories that will bring freedom. You carry so much wisdom in your hands that can connect people to the Father. I know there is fear in this. Remember that He has given you the power to set up boundaries over your life against all things hindering your voice from being heard. Don't just answer the call. Let Him develop you into the phone.

BONUS CHAPTERS

A CRYSTAL-CLEAR REFLECTION OF GOD WITHIN THE WORLD TODAY

Taking areas, I saw God use adversity to etch His perfect image
into my life and apply them to the etchings He is
making in the church today.

CHAPTER 13

CRYSTAL PAIN OF BEING CRUSHED

It was only a few weeks after Nathan passed away when one of my good friends, Susan Dollery, spoke a prophetic word over me. She told me I would write a book about my journey after losing Nathan and even proceeded to give me titles for the first three chapters. Susan has been a vessel for the voice of the Lord throughout many seasons of my life's journey.

I first met Susan during my youth, when I was struggling with an addiction to pain medication. I had driven to a Bible study, and I was sitting in my car trying to get the nerve to walk in. While sitting there, I popped the last of my pills. I prayed to God, telling Him I was so tired of the struggle. I said, "God, if people really do hear you speak, then tell them I need help. I'm too embarrassed to tell them how messed up I am, but I am so done with life."

I'll never forget how in the middle of that meeting, Susan said, "I feel like we need to pray for Cecily." I was shocked! I knew they couldn't tell I was high on pills because I had been taking them for years. At that point, the pills no longer got me high. They just kept me from being sick from withdrawals. I remember thinking, *Wow! God really does speak to people!* They sat me in what was referred

145

Crystal Pain

to as the "hot seat." It was a chair that they sat in the middle of the group. I thought this was a little odd, but I knew God was doing something. They gathered around me and started to pray. Susan prophesied over me, and at that moment, I was supernaturally set free from addiction. It was my first tangible encounter with the cleansing power of the Lord. I could feel something shift inside me when I physically witnessed His love through encouragement and edification flowing through His people. At that moment, I knew He knew me more than anyone and loved me despite all my errors. He never gave up on me. God tells us that we are beautifully and wonderfully made. We are created with a purpose. He will go to great lengths to see that through in our lives, no matter what comes against us. He uses it all to grow us, develop us, and guide us. This even includes those areas within our lives that we have walked in rebellion. If we allow Him to, He can use it to bring us to a greater awareness of who He is. He can use us to touch others' lives.

"All things work together for good to those who love God, to those who are called according to His purpose" (Romans 8:28, NKJV).

When Susan first gave me the prophetic word about writing this book, I grabbed hold of it with a tight grip. By this time in my life, I knew without a doubt that she had heard the voice of the Lord. In that desperate stage of my walk, that prophecy filled me with hope that one day this would all make sense. I could hear my husband's last words over me, "Minister out of OUR heart, now." That prophecy was something that told me, even in the gut-wrenching pain and absence of my other half, that God wanted to still use me. Just like He had shown me grace so many other times in my walk with Him, He would use this to not just bless me but to bless others.

Originally, I thought I was just going to write about how I saw God in the last days of my husband's battle with cancer. I thought maybe I would step into a place where I could be used to help set others free from the grips of grief. I thought that maybe I could be used to help them see the areas God was still there in their own stories. I felt strengthened to push forward and really tackle the heartbreak that accompanied grief. I read books on grief by C. S. Lewis and even watched TED Talks by those who overcame it. I thought, *I can do this!*

I think many times, we see great ministers of the gospel, and we ask God to use us like they are being used. We might even think because we have withstood many trials in life, it qualifies us to speak on the matter. What we fail to see is the amount of crushing that the people we are asking to be used have gone through. The crushing brought forth new wine in their lives.

God can give us spiritual gifts to use, place a calling on our lives, equip us with knowledge, and walk us through the fire. But it's our choice to submit wholeheartedly to Him. It's when we make up our minds to turn over these things to Him that He can use them to create that new wine. Think of it like grapes. They are an amazing fruit we can enjoy, but they must be crushed to bring forth the necessary substances before they can be turned into wine. If we submit our fruits (gifts, callings, and talents) to Him, He can use the trial to crush them and bring forth the perfect substance needed for a new wine to flow out of our life. After the crushing, there is a fermentation and purification process. Both crushing and cleansing are often needed before you can deliver revelation knowledge to others that will allow God's authentic refreshing to be consumed.

I wasn't aware of the extent of excruciating pain that accompanies this kind of crushing. I had already walked through several hardships in my life, but this was different from them all. I didn't realize what dying to your flesh truly felt like, what the cleansing of your soul required, or how I'd react to the ripping away of all

Crystal Pain

things I wrapped my identity around outside of God being at the core. I never thought that I'd find myself in the middle of a desert, stripped naked, full of agonizing pain, and then have temptation present itself. I always told God to take me to the darkest places so that I could help the lost. I never thought of the dark places looking like what I was experiencing. I definitely never thought I would cave to temptation and believe that there was no need to see the journey through to completion. I never imagined myself being someone in the middle of the darkness saying, "I've learned enough. I don't want to do this anymore."

I had to ask myself many times, will you continue to stand? And many times, I settled for the partiality of what I knew God could do. As you have seen in my story, I even succumbed to rebellion. I had to come to a place where I was willing to gain the wisdom that could be poured out by being in complete humility. Could I truly recognize that I am no one without God? Was I willing to submit to the transformation of Christlikeness? We are in control of nothing, but He gives much to those devoted to being a true servant of Christ. Was I ready for that? I want to say yes. But through my journey, I now know I can never brag about what "I" think my future holds but can only try to focus on Him daily. I have had my eyes open to how easily I, in my own might, can get off course. I now personally understand the need for total surrender, mercy, and the ever-important need for His grace. I understand that we are to take up our cross daily and what refusing to do so invites in our lives.

"If you refuse to take up your cross and follow me, you are not worthy of being mine. If you cling to your life, you will lose it; but if you give up your life for me, you will find it" (Matthew 10:38–39, NLT).

I am no different than many of God's people. I am aware of the word, have personally encountered the Lord's blessings in my

Crystal Pain of Being Crushed

life, been showered with His love, and undeservingly experienced being used as one of His vessels. But I fail so often. I've walked in pride, partnered with rebellion, placed the very blessings God gave me as idols, and even turned a blind eye to sin. Yet every time I repent, I've been met by Him with open arms. He not only invites me back into His family but gives me a seat at His table. How beautiful are His mercy and forgiveness! I know that the grace He extended to me is freely given to ALL. That is why we must always remain humble, never thinking we are better than anyone and truly want others to know that this invitation is freely extended to them too. I imagine there is assigned seating at His table, and He is just waiting to pull out the chair for the one whose name is on the place setting.

CHAPTER 14

CRYSTAL PAIN OF REPEATING HISTORY

I was reminded of the words God spoke to Abraham. God promised to make Abraham into a great nation.

"I will make you into a great nation, and I will bless you; I will make your name great, and you will be a blessing" (Genesis 12;2, NKJV).

God tells Abraham that He will bless him and make his descendants as numerous as the sand on the seashore. He said that ALL the nations on earth would be blessed because Abraham obeyed Him. Through Abraham's son (Jacob), the nation of Israel was formed. The Israelites were set apart and anointed by the Lord; however, they were not without struggle. They stepped into much rebellion, which led to unimaginable behaviors within their nation. Despite their struggles, God still wanted to bless them and even used them to bless ALL nations.

To be transformed into Christ's image, we need to walk in humility. We must be fully submitted to Him. I have discussed throughout this book areas in my own life that were unsubmitted to God and how humbling myself before Him brought me freedom from those things that were keeping me in great bondage. The opposite of humility is pride. It's that simple. I've highlighted in depth the many ways pride played a significant role in all my struggles. Whether that was unforgiveness, bitterness, jealousy, rebellion, anger, self-pity, or idolatry, all were rooted in pride. Pride is a hyper-focus on self. It might have been what I desired to gain, feeling sorry for myself, thinking I deserved something, or not wanting to give something up that I had possession of. These thought patterns opened me up to walking in partnership with pride.

Pride is one of the most powerful forces that Satan uses. After all, it was his inflated pride in himself and desire for power that got him kicked out of heaven, to begin with. That pride is what he has been using as a weapon ever since. It is what leads us into rebellion, and it is ultimately an unyielded desire for control he attempts to get us to partner with. I intensely discussed an example of these attempts while describing narcissistic attacks and even shared areas within my own journey, I succumbed to these influences. Narcissism is just a fancy word that is used today to describe great pride and control. The word itself was taken from a mythological figure named Narcissus. Narcissus was the one who was said to have fallen in love with his own reflection. I don't want to beat a dead horse, but I think there is a connection between Satan's hunger for control, power, and love of self and how he attempts to turn people away from God through history.

Many people in today's world have been able to pinpoint these deceptive ways while investigating narcissism. However, I believe it goes deeper than just a select pool of people within our society. Narcissism is just the tip of the iceberg. It's just the awareness of those spirits of pride in operation with one individual. When you study the nation of Israel's demise, you can start to see the enemy's deceptive plans on a grander scale. There have been repeating plans in operation for centuries. Is it possible that we have just been able to see a glimpse of them?

Crystal Pain of Repeating History

Israel was a nation anointed by God and used to bless all nations. Before we get to the good part, I want to highlight the cycle of pride they found themselves in. They were a chosen nation, set apart, and highly favored by God. In Psalm 105, we see that God made a covenant with them regarding their inheritance. He said that no one could touch them, for they were anointed, and He commanded no one to harm His prophets. Even with this covenant, they continued to fail and commit adultery on God by falling into idol worship and rebellion. You see, that is the trick. God said no one could touch them or harm them. There was a hedge of protection around them. For anything to get inside this hedge of protection, it required them to actively open a door of access. This is what Satan plotted to do. He attacked their minds and thought patterns by contaminating the truth with distorted lies. He played on their pride.

As I read through the Old Testament many times, I am baffled at the amount of chances God gives them. Just when you think they've finally gotten themselves together, they repeat the cycle. I thought to myself, if Israel was my covenant bride, I would divorce them. At one time, God Himself even does this. Of course, God always has a bigger picture in His playbook. I also knew that in my own life, I was greatly thankful for His patience and mercy to not divorce me. I knew there had to be a bigger picture and was determined to remain hopeful of seeing my story transpose.

Intrigued by Israel's cycle, I began to read it more and noticed something interesting. I saw that scriptures often discussed the destruction of the Leviathan directly before a cry to rescue Israel from their waywardness. Anytime Leviathan is mentioned, it was a season of idol worship, rebellion, confusion, and arrogance among the people. In Isaiah 27, we are told that Israel will be purged of all its wickedness, and the pagan altars will be crushed. It says that God will take His sword and punish the Leviathan, and on that day, they are to sing about the fruitful vineyard. Israel is this vineyard

Crystal Pain

(Psalm 80 and Isaiah 5).

Again, in Psalm 74, they speak of all the prophets being killed, and the places where God was worshipped were burned down. It then talks of crushing the head of Leviathan and letting the desert animals eat him. Israel cries out again, this time urging God to remember His covenant promises with the nation. I can relate so well to this. I've found myself in a time knowing I was rebelling, seeking control through my own desires, and when I experienced great spiritual warfare, I cried out to God to rescue me. I begged Him to remember I was a child of His!

While discussing narcissism, a controlling form of pride in a person, I told you I believe that the army behind this was under the leadership of the Leviathan Spirit. This belief stems directly from these correlations I found in God referencing Leviathan directly before discussing Israel and its rebellious corruption. In 1 Kings 21, Israel's rulers at that time, Ahab and Jezebel, ended up being eaten by desert animals along with all their descendants. This was their punishment for not yielding to the prophets' warning and killing them instead. I find it hard to think it's just a coincidence that Psalm 74 reiterates the fact that God crushed Leviathan and let the desert animals eat him. I have discussed Ahab and Jezebel's ways in great detail. You can reference those chapters if you need to refresh your memory. I want you to keep your focus on the nation of Israel.

Also, when I mention Leviathan, what I am referring to is the King of Pride in all its forms. I don't want people to get lost in this message because of a name they might not be familiar with. I merely studied the Leviathan because I saw patterns of this name being mentioned over and over and how it follows a pattern of corruption and prideful ways. However, the focus here should be how pride itself is often disguised and used in bringing about destructive ways. Again, I am no expert in demonology and truly am not

Crystal Pain of Repeating History

concerned with what people want to call specific things. I simply saw patterns at work through the scripture. Also, there were many kings in Israel, and Ahab was just one. Since we have discussed him in-depth, and you have a quick reference to refresh your memory on Ahab's ways, I have decided to keep with his story.

Israel often fell into idol worship. One of the false gods they worshipped, and one that stood true during Ahab's rule, was Baal.

"Israel did evil in the Lord's sight and served the images of Baal" (Judges 2:11 NLT)

Worshipping Baal included child sacrifices, astrology, witchcraft, sexual sin, and prostitution (2 Kings 23:5, Jeremiah 19:5, 2 Kings 9:22, Revelation 2:20). These scriptures include accounts of them burning their children at altars, incense offered to the moon and stars, prostitution, and committing sexual acts. By this time, Israel was in such a state of confusion and rebellion they rejected the commandments of God.

The prophet Ezekiel describes one of the many cycles Israel was in. He shows how God took Israel when it was found abandoned and neglected, and He saved it. He tells us how God washed it clean and gave it much beauty and blessings. In return, Israel used all these blessings and gifts to build idols. They used these gifts, beauty, and blessings for selfish gain. During this round, they committed prostitution and used their beauty to gain money, as well as entice others to do the same acts. Ezekiel emphasizes how Israel forgot how it felt to be left abandoned and neglected as a child, and now they are offering their own children as sacrifices. They were clouded by selfish pride.

(See Journal Entry "Distorted Body Image" on page 222)

While studying Leviathan (Pride), I saw it referenced as the python, the coiling or twisting serpent, a monster of the sea. It was spoken of as one that tries to close the womb of woman or a

Crystal Pain

dragon that set out to make wroth with the remnant of her seed. Satan himself was often symbolized as a serpent or a dragon. I'm not opposing the possibility that Leviathan is another symbol of Satan. I am not certain. What I do know is that it was evil and demonic, and there was a connection intertwined throughout the continuous fall of Israel. This was enough information to solidify within me my assumption regarding Satan using an army led by pride. He twisted God's truth, getting Israel to rebel and birth a controlling nature within them. Satan used pride, in all its disguises, to dethrone God and told them that they could gain anything that they wanted through sources outside of God. It showed me that Satan was using it to not only get God's people to rebel against His commands, but they were destroying their own nation by sacrificing their offspring. This confusion that clouded their judgment was allowing Satan to use them like his puppets. They themselves were killing off the chosen remnant, along with their descendants. Remember, these were the very people God had designed to carry forth a call to bless ALL the nations of the world.

After reading these multiple accounts in the scriptures, I started to reflect on our world today. Were there any areas in our lives today where we can see any of these acts of idolatry? Was history repeating itself? I knew that within my own life's story, I recognized how Satan was never creative and often used things I had struggled with in my past and reinserted that same prideful struggle when he found me confused. I knew in my life's story, I was able to see the workings that lined up with characteristics of pride, like those of Jezebel and Ahab. Like many others in the world today, I, too, was able to see the deceptions at work in narcissism. There was an influx of self-satisfaction and self-focus. If you are wondering what some of these are, Galatians tells us the cravings of that self-life are obvious.

Crystal Pain of Repeating History

The cravings of the self-life are obvious: sexual immorality, lustful thoughts, pornography, chasing after things instead of God, manipulating others, hate of those that get in your way, senseless arguments, resentment when others are favored, temper tantrums, angry quarrels, only thinking of yourself, being in love with your own opinion, being envious of the blessings of others, murder, uncontrolled addictions, wild parties, and all the similar behaviors.

Galatians 5:20 (TPT)

We saw these examples in Israel, but could I see other ways our world today had been walking in a parallel manner as Israel? Especially when they stepped into the idol worship of Baal?

I asked myself, in today's world, are there any accounts of child sacrifice? Did I recognize any increased use of astrology and fixation on the moon and stars for answers? Could I see people using their beauty and appearance to gain influence or money, as well as enticing others to do the same? Were there any areas in our lives where we were taking the blessings that God gave us and turning them into an idol? Was there any sexual immorality that was being widely accepted?

I do not know how you chose to answer these questions, but as for myself, I answered yes to them all. In this reflection, I stumbled across a story about a famous fortune-teller that often predicted events that happened regarding our own U.S. government. I don't feel it necessary to even mention her name, but many may remember who I am about to discuss. She predicted the assassination of JFK and was often consulted by other U.S. presidents. She called herself a prophetess but used crystal balls and practices that lined up with more of a New Age style. Stumbling across this knowl-

Crystal Pain

edge felt like a pit in my stomach.

I learned that she wrote a book, and within this book, she describes an encounter she had one night as she was sleeping. She says that there was a serpent that crawled into her bed and wrapped itself around her. When this serpent looked into her eyes, she says that she felt like she received all-knowing wisdom and felt such peace, and that light illuminated her room. How could our very own nation be one that allowed such a twisted version of truth into its place of authority? I was always told that we called ourselves a Christian nation. Our very own currency has "In God, We Trust" written on it. This fortune-teller lined up with the exact description of a false prophet. How could they not see this?

Did we as Christians not understand that fortunetelling is not the workings of our God? I'm not saying there isn't supernatural power behind it. I believe that Satan does, in fact, have supernatural powers. But it is not the power of God, and we know that God's power and authority have dominion over all of it. Satan's power can carry truth. He uses this truth but twists and distorts it. He disguised himself as light. The name Lucifer even means "light bearer." He uses this counterfeit light. If he can get us to put our guard down, he knows we will open ourselves up to counterfeits, and then he can bring in destruction. Reading about the use of this kind of witchcraft in our nation's history was heartbreaking!

In Acts, there is a story of Paul and his companions traveling to Macedonia. This is where they were met by a slave woman who was earning a lot of money for her masters through fortune telling.

"One day, as we were going to the house of prayer, we encountered a young slave girl who had an evil spirit of divination, the spirit of Python. She had earned great profits for her owners by being a fortune-teller" (Acts 16:16, TPT).

Paul tells us how she followed them around for days shouting how they were the great servants of The Most High God and they

Crystal Pain of Repeating History

were telling people how to be saved. Paul eventually got agitated by this and turns around and commands the spirit inside her to come out, in Jesus' name. That spirit left her, and her masters were upset because they knew they would no longer be able to make money with her. The spirit that was working in her, the one that they referred to as the Python and divination, was what allowed her to tell fortunes. You see, this woman was speaking the truth. Paul and his companions were, in fact, servants of God and teaching on salvation, but she was not operating out of the pure power of God. Paul recognized this counterfeit. Once he rebuked this spirit, she lost all her abilities. The Holy Spirit of the Lord flowing through Paul trumped any other spirit and gave him authority to command it to leave. God's power in us is always more powerful than any power Satan has, and through the Holy Spirit, we, too, have been given the ability to discern the difference.

It would be easy for me to condemn the world for all these acts of idolatry. It would be easy to point fingers and place criticism on them. I could allow hate to come into my heart. Fortunately, that isn't how I initially felt when I first had this realization. Yes, it hurts my heart that I can see how people have turned from our loving God. There is room for righteous anger if it is accompanied by a greater love. But I also can see more than anything that wounded, unhealed orphan. And I remembered that if Israel could be used to bring ALL to inherit the blessings of the Lord, our nation, too, could be used in this very way.

I thought there must be something inside them that has not truly accepted their adoption into a family, and they couldn't see the overwhelming love our Father has for them. There is something that is blinding them from seeing this. I can remember the feeling of desperation while walking in sinful ways, the cloud of confusion when you feel like you don't belong anywhere, and the striving to find a place you fit. There is an offense that arises when you feel so misunderstood, and a battle against shame quickly turns to

Crystal Pain

rebellion. You can get so far down the wrong path that you fail to see which way is up, grabbing hold of anything that seems like it carries unity. No matter what the power source is behind it, you just grasp for having a voice that others are willing to hear. You cry out for attention, something that says I see you, and you matter. I also know, through my experience, no matter what you portray, there is a lack of peace living this lifestyle. Eventually, you require more and more to fill the void. This alone should make compassion rise up inside us, as believers, toward all walking this blind path. There should be a yearning inside us to want all to encounter the true purity of our loving Father.

I can't believe that God is going to give up on us as a nation. Just like the Israelite nation, He wants to see us all come to repent and step into our rightful role as His chosen sons and daughters. He wants us to see and understand the glorious inheritance we gain in sonship. He is not giving up on us, just as He didn't give up on Israel. But I do believe He is highlighting the overwhelming need for us to go out and reach the lost.

CHAPTER 15

CRYSTAL PAIN OF THE BEAST

When reading the 7th chapter in the book of Daniel, you see him describing four beasts that came up from the sea. I will not attempt to interpret the meaning behind the beasts, but what I want to focus on is how this vision ends. It states that in the end, there was a judgment made in favor of the saints.

"And a judgment was made in favor of the saints of the Most High, and the time came for the saints to possess the kingdom" (Daniel 7:22, NKJV).

Praise God! He tells us that the beast will be destroyed FOR-EVER and that ALL will serve and obey God. I love it when I hear believers talking about the Bible, and they say they know how the book ends. We win! The book of Daniel is not the only place we see this beast spoken of. The book of Revelation, the end of the Bible (the book), speaks of this same beast referenced again. It says that it rose out of the sea and often said it spoke like a dragon, and the dragon gave this beast its authority. Revelation chapter 14 tells us that, for a period of time, this beast would be given author-ity and that many would follow it. We are told that there would be great signs and wonders it performs, there would be false prophets

Crystal Pain

in this time, and that these would contribute to the deception of the world and the reason why they turn to follow the "beast." I was identifying things within our world again. I saw the deception that was covering people's eyes and the use of false prophets that had been consulted throughout history. Jezebel herself called herself a prophetess, and even a few years back, within our own U.S., we had a false prophetess trying to consult with our presidents. They used great signs and wonders and displayed supernatural powers, although their source was not God.

In this same chapter, we see the mentioning of the "mark" of the beast. Even though there are numerous theories revolving around this, most Christians are familiar with it in one aspect or another. Again, I am not going to try and interpret the meaning behind the beast itself. Its description alone (beast of the sea and voice of the dragon) was enough to determine it was our enemy. But like many other Christians, I have found myself curious about the "mark of the beast." Intrigued about this, I decided to study it a little more in-depth. Through studying the *Strong's Concordance*, I discovered that the word marked (engraved) in Greek carries the same root word from which we get the word "Character." That's interesting! So, one might say, "The Mark of the Beast" could be rephrased as "The Character of the Beast." Looking at the next statement, Revelations says that the beast caused everyone, great and small, rich and poor, free and bound, to be marked on the right hand and the forehead.

I have mentioned my love for symbolism and how I love to see the deeper meaning throughout the Bible while researching the symbolism behind various words. I began to look at the mark of the beast from a different perspective when it says they will be marked on the forehead and their right arm. The forehead symbolically stands for our thoughts and reasoning of the mind. It is taking on the evil characteristics of the enemy within our own internal belief structures. We see when describing the fall of a false religious

Crystal Pain of the Beast

system Satan tried to use to destroy God's people a description that is marked on "her" head.

"A mysterious name was written on her forehead: Babylon the great, Mother of All Prostitutes, and Obscenities in the World" (Revelations 17:5, NLT).

This mark seems to describe the distorted workings of evil within the world. Let's take a closer look at the right hand. Hands symbolize our actions. This passage could specifically refer to those actions that follow after we come into agreement with these evil thoughts. I see it as our thoughts become distorted, confused, and filled with corruption allowing our actions to become influenced and follow those characteristics of evil ways. Those obscene ways were reflected throughout Israel's rebellion, especially in Babylon.

Would these characteristics be what marked us as being under the rule and reign of this "beast"? These characteristics follow man's ways, not God's. The number six is the number of men. I find it hard to believe that there will actually be the number 666 stamped on people's foreheads and hands. Being able to recognize the mark of the beast will require the wisdom and discernment that comes from total submission to the Holy Spirit. If this mark was something we could physically recognize, like a number tattooed on people, we would not need to be in submission to the Holy Spirit to discern it. I believe recognizing it will require us to take our thoughts and actions and place them under the Holy Spirit's guidance. It will require us to actively be followers and worshippers of God.

What could these thoughts be? What would the distorted truths be rooted in? If our thoughts need to be reflective of God, what do the thoughts of evil look like?

There was a Christian monk and one of the most influential theologians in the late fourth-century church named Evagrius Ponticus. At one point, he spent time alone in the desert, searching

Crystal Pain

to greater understand Jesus's own walk in the desert. We know that when Jesus found Himself in the desert, He was faced with the accusation of Satan and had His identity tested. Jesus came up against many lies that were designed to test His thoughts and beliefs. He had to cling to God's Word and fight with the truth held within the scripture.

Evagrius when to the desert and had intended to follow Jesus's example while walking in the wilderness. Don't get me wrong, from any standpoint. I can see how this can sound a little far-fetched. You would think that whatever he discovered had to come from a strange viewpoint after spending that much time in the heat of the desert. However, his discoveries were extremely interesting, nonetheless. Evagrius wrote a short book called *Talking Back: A Monastic Handbook for Combating Demons*. In this book, he wasn't writing to the general public but to other monks. He discussed eight evil thoughts and how they contributed to interferences within their spiritual practices. These thoughts revolved around gluttony, lust, avarice, anger, sloth, sadness, vainglory, and pride.

One of Evagrius's students brought these ideas to the Western church. In the sixth century, St. Gregory the Great (Pope Gregory I) rearranged them into his commentary on the book of Job. Pope Gregory I removed "sloth" and added "envy," and instead of giving "pride" its own place on the list, he described it as the ruler of the other seven vices. This went on to become known as the familiar Seven Deadly Sins. They were called deadly because committing one of these sins was said to bring death to the soul. Other theologians revisited these Seven Deadly Sins throughout the centuries, and all would contribute "pride" as the leading ruler over the other seven sins.

In the book *Live No Lies* by John Mark Comer, it states, "Evagrius generated the most sophisticated demonology of ancient Christianity. And the most surprising feature of Evagrius's paradigm is his claim that the fight against demonic temptation is a fight against what he called *logismoi*—a Greek word that can translate as "thoughts," "thought patterns" your "internal narratives," or "internal belief structures."

If I haven't lost you by now, you might be asking yourself, *Why is she telling us this story about a monk who went out into the desert to fight the devil?* I find it interesting that his findings were so great of an influence that they are still being referenced by theologians today. We see the need to take all thoughts captive and how pride is the root of all other sins. There is strong proof that our thoughts and belief structures give way to our actions. These principles are taught to us throughout scripture. It all points back to not allowing our thoughts to become saturated with self. Not giving way to thoughts revolving around anything that starts with self. Some examples are self-made, self-motive, self-righteous, self-pity, self-harm, and self-serving. You get the picture. Pride is a grandiose focus on self, which leads to a lack of needing God, and placing power in idolatry of other sources. It leads to rebellion, confusion, and all other forms of corruption. I have gone as far as to say it's the primary weapon Satan uses in his attempts to destroy God's people.

Is this where Israel went wrong? Did they come to a place within their walk with God where they stopped saying God, how can we serve you, and switched it to God, how can you serve us? I can imagine them taking God's ways and trying to get Him to move on their behalf by using this works-driven mindset. I actually think we all can get to this point in our lives if we aren't careful. We understand God's power and how it flows in various ways and think that following a simple pattern or process will gain us a reward.

Maybe it is finding yourself sick and praying a certain prayer daily, taking communion daily, or using anointing oils with the goal of obtaining your healing placed higher than glorifying God. Your focus is directed on the outcome you desire more than the goodness of God. I've been here. When my husband was sick, I reached for anything that would bring us the healing I knew God said we had a right to. I played worship music nonstop, took communion, fasted, and read scriptures I had taped up daily. But at times, I was using them like magic, just like Israel's biggest mistake. I began to think that the promise was in the works versus God Himself. If you remember, I was the one (not my husband) who got angry and yelled out at God, "Where are you?" and "Why are you not moving?"

(See Journal Entry "Seeds of Confusion" on page 267)

I wonder if Israel found themselves like this and quickly turned to other gods because they grew angry waiting on God to move. They were impatient, grew rebellious, and stopped seeking Him out of a place of true submission and a servant's heart. The book of Romans breaks down how Israel believed that through their own works, they could become righteous. They allowed their internal beliefs to get hijacked by self-righteousness, and their thoughts were distorted. Paul then references Elijah. He speaks about the time he was hiding after Jezebel and Ahab killed all the prophets besides him. Elijah comes to God in fear for his life. God answered him by assuring him that he was not alone. God spoke of a group of faithful followers who refused to bow down to the worship of Baal. He tells us that it was God's grace that empowered this body of believers. This is where we get to the good part.

This is where we start to see the need for a Redeemer, a Savior. One who was spotless and without sin. This is where we are told about Jesus! The one who would bear all our sins and bring us freedom from the law. He speaks about how even the Gentiles (non-Jews) would now be grafted into the family of God and receive the inheritance. There was an adoption that took place and death to the feeling that anyone was left out, didn't belong, or didn't fit. Through faith and God's grace, ALL would be blessed. It was this very grace that was extended to all that would give Israel the ability to come back to God.

"A partial and temporary hardening to the gospel has come over Israel, which will last until the full number of non-Jews has come into God's family. And then God will bring all of Israel to salvation!" (Romans 11:25–26, TPT)

This is the gospel; this is the good news! We all now have access to it. It is freely given and only requires our submission to God. We are merely responsible for taking our thoughts captive, submitting them to the Lord, and of course, helping others see the simplicity of walking under this powerful love.

CHAPTER 16

CRYSTAL PAIN OF DISCERNING THE BODY

It's easy to notice an influential minister or hear a powerful sermon and say to God, "I want to be used like that." We may be willing to undergo the testing, pruning, and crushing that accompanies gaining wisdom to hold such a position. But do we, as a nation, want to be used like Israel? A nation that was anointed by God and attacked greatly by the enemy? Are we able to stand in the gap as a chosen family of believers to bring the good news to the rest of the nation? Are we prepared for that type of crushing?

We can look at our world today and see the works of Satan. We might recognize similarities with our nation that are parallel with those that Israel was walking in. Just as God told the chosen remnant, they cannot ever think that they are better than anyone else, we, too, need to keep our hearts humble and full of love. We also need to make sure that if we are judging others, we are not without fault ourselves.

"You hypocrites, first take the plank out of your own eye, and then you will see clearly to remove the speck from your brother's eye" (Matthew 7:5, NLT).

We can get hyper-focused on the evil that surrounds our world

Crystal Pain

and falls into fear. We can try and figure out if we are in the last days. Many feel the need to prepare for the worst by taking their money out of the banks, stockpiling supplies, loading up on weapons and ammo, and storing food. I am not condemning any of this. I only want to make sure that we are giving just as much attention to preparing our souls. We need to make sure that we are walking in humility, laying down all forms of pride, and properly preparing our family for war against evil. This includes our own family members as well as all those within our church family. Remember, as the world continues to get more and more evil, we are in a war against the principalities of darkness. We need to be giving just as much of our energy to preparing to fight in the spiritual realm. Throughout the passage of Psalm 4, it repeatedly says, "pause in His presence" prior to instruction on how to handle the battle at hand.

God's instruction is to offer a righteous sacrifice of trust and meditate on our sins and repent. I believe He says this in order to take our focus off the attack and back onto our soul. There is an internal battle at hand that we should be just as aware of. We cannot battle spiritual attacks with fleshly instincts. God sees our submission to Him (through trust) as a righteous sacrifice and our denying of flesh as an offering to Him that is holy. Our job is to rid ourselves of anything we have in common with the spiritual things attacking our world. This is the only way they lose their grip on altering our peace and instilling chaos into our lives.

We need to actively remember to take time to rest and search our souls. We cannot control the world around us, but we can control what we allow inside our hearts. We can be used to be a witness to others and be a carrier of God's love for all. We should be constantly aware of denying fleshly reactions, whether it is taking offense, becoming bitter, carrying unforgiveness, slander, blaming others, or fighting fire with fire. Also, don't fear trial. One of the biggest fears in life is pain and discomfort during a trial. However,

Crystal Pain of Discerning the Body

God is closest to us in times of pain. With struggle comes birthing, breakthrough, guidance, humility, discipline, and growth. He will use it all.

He comes to fight our battles for us if we submit and humble ourselves before Him. We are called to release good into this world, and He is a hedge of protection around us from anything altering that good. If we find ourselves facing anxiety, God releases peace. If we find ourselves facing hate, He releases love. If it's indiscipline, He releases self-control. If it's sorrow, He releases joy. Our job is just to choose our weapons wisely. One will invoke weariness and the other rest. Release what has freely been given to you through God taking up residence inside you. We must learn to fight in rest!

Our world is in desperate need of healing. Whether that healing is within our own souls, physical healing, or mental illness. These things were never God's will for our lives. God's will for our lives is for good and not for disaster. He wants to give us a future and hope. He will bring justice. My anticipation is that this justice will be a return to God's kingdom for most.

Unfortunately, I know that not all will turn back, and when God separates the goats from the sheep, many will be the goats. Our job is to prepare the sheep, to heal their heart, to show them what Agape love looks like in the flesh, and to continue to ask the Father to open our eyes and the Holy Spirit to give us discernment and wisdom. This will require training ourselves to not have to fear and allow it to overshadow the truth. God is for us and not against us. He has empowered us, and He has given us an assignment.

> *A house divided against itself cannot stand. I believe this government cannot endure, permanently half-slave and half-free. I do not expect the union to be dissolved — I do not expect the house*

Crystal Pain

to fall — but I do expect it will cease to be divided. It will become all one thing or all the other.

Abraham Lincoln

I find this quote from our sixteenth president interesting. Taking it from a biblical perspective, this "house divided" quote originated from the gospels within the New Testament. President Lincoln was speaking of slavery within our U.S., but I would like to point out the slavery that is still going on. There are those who have been set free by the saving grace of Jesus and those who are still bound to darkness. We've been given a great commission to go out and set the captives free. Many know that they are called to the mission field and the marketplace, and this is a beautiful assignment for all. It is something that we do not need to take lightly. I think it is important to understand; however, this assignment doesn't just include going out and getting people to come to church. Many times, we think if we can get them to church, then we can just put them in the hands of our pastors, and our job is finished.

In Exodus 18, we see Moses being instructed as a pastor to empower others to help him with the judging and ministering duties. He was told that he couldn't do it all on his own or would wear himself out. You see, God has instructed the church body to play a role in loving, helping mature, and saving the people within the house, just as much as touching the people outside the house. This responsibility is not just on our pastors. If the church is going to come up against the darkness of the world, we need to be healthy. As the saying goes, it takes a village.

If we have a church that is composed of those living in freedom, and those who are still held captive, we are still a house divided. Unfortunately, we also see members attacking each other and not walking in the union. If we are called the body of Christ, is this not like an autoimmune disease? It does not make sense when a body cries out for healing yet at the same time continues

Crystal Pain of Discerning the Body

to attack itself.

First Corinthians 11 talks about communion. Paul says the reason why we are weak, sickly, and dying prematurely is because we are told to discern the Lord's body; nevertheless, we fail to do so.

> *So, then whoever eats the bread or drinks the cup of the Lord in a way that is unworthy [of Him] will be guilty of [profaning and sinning against] the body and blood of the Lord. But a person must [prayerfully] examine himself [and his relationship to Christ], and only when he has done so should he eat of the bread and drink of the cup. For anyone who eats and drinks [without solemn reverence and heartfelt gratitude for the sacrifice of Christ], eats and drinks a judgment on himself if he does not recognize the body [of Christ]. That [careless and unworthy participation] is the reason why many among you are weak and sick, and a number sleep [in death]. But if we evaluated and judged ourselves honestly [recognizing our shortcomings and correcting our behavior], we would not be judged. But when we [fall short and] are judged by the Lord, we are disciplined [by undergoing His correction] so that we will not be condemned [to eternal punishment] along with the world.*

1 Corinthians 27–32 (AMPC)

After reading this passage, I know for myself I was convicted of the many times I failed to examine my own soul and humble myself before the Lord prior to participating in communion. Then I became stirred in my spirit for those within my own church that might not understand the overwhelming love and grace Father God has for them and the magnitude of what Jesus did on the cross for them. I had so many questions running through my mind. Were the

Crystal Pain

unsaved within my own church truly aware of the power behind communion? Had I done my part in showing the same love to everyone I encountered, to be a vessel of God to shower them with this love? Did I carry any ought against my fellow believers within the church that I failed to lay down? Was I discerning the body of Christ broken for me as well as the body of Christ (the church) I had called my home?

I knew I asked the Lord to make me a vessel to heal the sick, to help bind up the broken, to reach the lost, but my eyes were closed shut to those that surrounded me weekly during Sunday service. I was guilty of walking past a new member. I was guilty of getting irritated with a fellow believer for not behaving in a manner I thought was righteous, and more than anything, I was guilty of not actively doing my part to change any of this by operating through and with God's love.

(See Journal Entry "Why Are Things Taking So Long"
on page 242)

About a month prior to this realization, I had been given the opportunity to help serve the homeless community hot meals. When I offered to help, I'll be honest, I just knew I had gotten to a place in my healing journey and that it was time for me to stop receiving and start serving again. I thought the least I could do was serve food to someone in need, be kind, and show them they were seen by others. It was an easy way to just show those in hard times a little love.

I began to become familiar with the people who showed up and even started to learn their names. We'd have conversations, and many would make me laugh with their stories. They walked with a positive outlook most days, and I realized quickly many were no different than myself. Had I not had a support system and family around many times in my life, this could have very well been a lifestyle I would have been forced to live.

Crystal Pain of Discerning the Body

As the weeks progressed, I got invited to go out to deliver the meals to the areas these individuals lived. I remember the first time I just stood there and cried; I was of no help at all. I had no idea these individuals I was building a relationship with living in the manner they did. It was right here in the small little town I lived in. Their homes were composed of three to seven tents deep within the wooded areas. They had their places nicely set up with chairs and laundry areas and would sit around talking as families. Many even had pets they took care of.

The part that was like a dagger through my heart came a few Sundays after this experience. When service was over, I was walking out of the church sanctuary when I ran into two of these people I had gotten to develop a relationship with. They had been coming to MY church the entire time! I had no idea that these individuals were MY family! They were part of the body, and prior to my serving, I had not been discerning them. Although I was so excited to see them, I felt overwhelming repentance come over me. It was truly an eye-opening experience.

When times start to look dark, we can get so hyper-focused on ourselves and how we might suffer if there is an apocalypse. Some say they are preparing so they can provide for others if things get bad. But the truth is, our job never changes. Why wait until the world ends to do that very thing? There are suffering people right in front of us now. We all probably can think of someone. It could be hurting children, families in turmoil, homeless communities, broken hearts, or even someone suffering from mental illness.

You don't have to go on a mission trip to Africa or into the inner cities of the U.S. Although, there is great training you can receive when you come under the leadership of others who have knowledge in these areas. However, I pray that you can mindfully be aware of the people you walk past on a weekly basis. The ones you know are suffering yet never make time in your schedule to

Crystal Pain

reach, or the new people at church you've never seen before. I know for a fact; it doesn't take much. Maybe it's like me and just scooping food onto someone's plate. Maybe it's a quick phone call, text, or card sent to someone in need of encouragement. It could even be as simple as a smile and "good morning" to someone you pass in the church halls.

Some plant seeds, and others water them, but it takes the entire body working together, doing their part. Sometimes we look at others' gifts and think to ourselves, "I don't have as great of a gift as them." It's easy to think you don't have anything within you that will make a difference. But God will flow through you right where you are. We are told to look at the church body just as we would a physical body; some members are eyes, some are ears, some are hands, etc. God has carefully designed each member and placed them within the body to function in a unique and specific way. God even says that the weaker the part, the more essential it is. I love that He flows through our weaknesses.

When my husband and I got married, we loved the fact that we became one in Spirit with the Lord at our center. There was such a strength that came to me, knowing that we had become a three-strand cord wrapped together as one flesh with the Lord.

"A person standing alone can be attacked and defeated, but two can stand back-to-back and conquer. Three are even better, for a triple-braided cord is not easily broken" (Ecclesiastes 4:12, NLT).

Our marriage required continually growing together, working on our communication, holding each other accountable, and humbly submitting to each other in love. We, the church, are the Bride of Christ. Just like my and my husband's marriage, we, as the Church, are yoked as one with Christ. This includes ALL the church members. Yes, even the ones that rub us wrong. Those areas that surface in frustrating times are areas we need to actively be aware of. By recognizing them, we can then invite the Lord into

Crystal Pain of Discerning the Body

that area for healing. This could be you recognizing something within another member that needs love and prayer or maybe even something within your own soul that still needs to be healed. We should always be actively working toward the inner healing that needs to take place within our church body.

When you are in a healthy personal relationship with someone, you often find yourself wanting to talk to them often. You share your dreams, struggles, and celebrations. You desire their feedback, guidance, and support. Something about them brings peace after visiting, and your spirits are lifted. The more time you spend with them, the more you feel closer to them. By learning how their lives shaped who they are, you can see their character displayed and the things that will remain constant in their personalities. Trust starts to develop in authenticity. You can find yourself giving to them, not because you want something in return, but because they have been such a blessing to you. You start putting them first and making time for them without thought. You can even find they make you want to become a better person.

Our personal relationship with Jesus should be the same as this. The more it becomes like this, the more it spills over onto those people within our lives.

So many times in my life, I have found myself in bondage to things, unable to break free in my own might. God has always led me to a place where I encountered a group of people that helped walk me through these trials. He either supernaturally flowed through them, and I experienced freedom instantaneously, or He brought mentors alongside me to help walk me through an intensive training season. However He chose to get me there, one fact remained, I needed community. I needed fellow believers and the power of the Lord flowing through them in whatever unique manner they were gifted to possess.

God used their unique journeys through life and allowed them

177

Crystal Pain

to gain wisdom through it. They just recognized a need within me and graciously poured that wisdom, covered with God's love, on me. In one capacity or another, I can only hope to be this for someone else. Even if it's just one.

MY JOURNAL THROUGH GRIEF

I have included these journal entries to highlight how God was speaking to me throughout the entire process. God is the Master Craftsman, etching His beautiful image into our lives through every circumstance. Some of God's etchings are deep, while others are just polishing up rough areas. He never stops walking alongside us. The enemy tries to blind us, still our joy, kill our vision, and make us turn to other things for comfort. As for me, I was able to hear His voice, but my heart was hardened to fully receive the revelation. Once I repented, submitted to Him, and was reconnected to my community of believers, I was able to see a clear groove He was etching in my journey the entire time. Then, the wisdom He was pouring out throughout the years took root in my soul, and healing came. I pray that you, too, will find the strength to write through your journey. My hope is that by sharing my story, it helps your healing journey come with a little more ease.

My Journal Through Grief

YEAR ONE

Crystal Pain

THE LOSS OF A BRIDE

Journal Entry

February 19th, 2020

Today marks two weeks Nathan has been in his glorified body. Today, I didn't want to get up. I didn't care about this life or anything that used to excite me. I only wanted to feel his embrace. I just wanted to hear his encouraging words and know I was safe. I prayed to God:

"Help me! Give me strength. You don't know what it's like to be alone. You've never lost like this. You have everything!"

I was reminded God had lost a son. And I responded, "It's not the same as a lifelong partner. My other half! How could you?"

In a calm, sweet voice, I hear Him whispering. "Did you forget you are my bride? And so many others, too. Don't give up! I KNOW your pain. Help me reach my lost members of my bride. Those who have yet an understanding of true authentic love. I know this hurt you feel, for I grieve, too."

Members of the Bride of Christ, I ask you to help me today. Let's help Christ, in some way, find His other half He's lost. It hurts so much to not be whole. It's the least we can do. Be kind, show generosity, and lend a helping hand. Be Jesus to one of His bride members who may be lost.

Have you ever questioned if God truly understands your struggle?

My Journal Through Grief

Where in the Word can you find examples of Him experiencing similar pain?

How can you actively reach the lost today?

Crystal Pain

I WILL STEWART ALL I GAINED

Journal Entry

February 25th, 2020

I roll over each morning and reach for Nathan's hand. Only to find it wasn't a dream, and he is really gone. That side of the bed is cold and empty. I ache stronger than a knife wound. People try and console me without knowing. It only drives the knife deeper. Sayings like, "You're young, and you'll find love again," hurt so bad because Nathan isn't replaceable. He was my answered prayers. With these prayers, so many people stood in agreement with me, believing I'd find someone like him. He was my best friend, my other half, my comfort, and my cheerleader. He was the one whom my soul loved.

I hear people say, "God is your husband now," but wasn't God my husband when Nathan was alive too? God doesn't replace my longing to be held by Nathan and lay in bed cracking up until we cry at the corny jokes we tell each other. God doesn't replace the feeling of Nathan's hand grab mine during worship, and even after almost a decade, I still got butterflies.

I am not alone, yes, this is true. I have people praying for me, and I am so very thankful. God doesn't leave of forsake me. That is true. But it doesn't take away the cold room at night. It doesn't take away the empty recliner where he sat, and I would crawl into his lap at the end of each day. The absence of text message he sent to me every morning for eight years saying he loved me and I was going to have a good day. My days are filled with emptiness! I have a broken, ripped heart that won't stop hurting even when I am wearing a fake smile that everything is okay. It hurts!

I understand, I will lose friends because I haven't "MOVED ON." As if my husband was just disposable, and I'm Debbie Downer now. I'd guess you haven't lost your spouse. It's not the same as a parent, uncle, or grandparent. Although that hurts tremendously, it's different!

I promised Nathan on his deathbed that I'd not lose my joy. I promised that I'd minister out of OUR heart now and continue to keep my faith. Even with all my hurt, I have not lost hope. That hope of Jesus healing our land and His return. When I get opportunities to love others, it's the only time the hurting stops, and my body is filled with refreshing strength and joy.

I think we have become confused about what it means to "receive" Jesus as our Lord and Savior. Jesus isn't something that fulfills our earthly desires. Yes, He is with us, and He loves us. He works things for our good, but the gifts He gives us aren't for us! He was not focused on self. You encounter God and His love by giving! Giving LOVE. Giving JOY. Giving PEACE. Giving KINDNESS, GOODNESS, GENTLENESS. The fruit was never for us to eat. It was to give away.

You see, God's gifts are often not about us. It's what submitting and dying to self are all about. The more you die to your flesh, humble yourself, and focus on others; the more you are filled with His glorious strength, which is JOY. If you have never ministered to someone outside the four walls of the church, I challenge you to. Maybe it's helping someone carry something, opening a door, pray-

Crystal Pain

ing for someone, making a meal, or paying for someone's tab at a restaurant. Whatever it is, I guarantee you that feeling you get after doing something good that's God's joy. It's the reward, and it's encountering God in the flesh.

Many might not know, but Nathan's name means "Gift from God." And even though he often made our life about me, in retrospect, his coming into my life as a gift from God was never about me. I will steward all I gained from our life; I will give out of the pain because I desire to encounter God! In some strange way, know all I was given through Nathan; I am supposed to give away.

What are some of the gifts you received through your loved ones?

_____

_____

_____

_____

_____

How can you continue to steward these gifts?

_____

_____

_____

_____

_____

My Journal Through Grief

RECOGNIZE THE LIES OF THE ENEMY

Journal Entry

March 8th, 2020

This world looks dark, but God is redirecting us back to the cross. Reminding us of our triumph over sin through Him. He reminds us of our authority gained over the grip and bondage sin once had. He is realigning us. He is releasing fresh assignments and adding vision to our previous call.

Many have gone through a fresh battle, coming out disoriented, wounded, and lacking clarity on their next steps.

Satan used this battle to try to place lies in our minds and get us to partner with new and old unhealthy strongholds. God is reminding us; Satan and sin have no power over us. Come back to Him. Let Him refresh HOPE in your heart. Let Him reveal to you the new character developed within you. Let Him reveal his overpowering Love that no wall or scar can prevent from penetrating. Soak in Him today and allow vision to be birthed.

Two thousand and twenty is just beginning, and God is preparing an ARMY. You may have been hit by the first blow, BUT God equips you with endurance, and you're wearing humility like a badge of honor which allows a massive download of wisdom for what's next. Just lock arms with the Father who loves you. He will guide your every step. He will have the victory, and He's choosing you to play a starring role.

Crystal Pain

Can you recognize any patterns you've reconnected with?

_____

_____

_____

_____

_____

What lie are you believing that has caused you to lose hope?

_____

_____

_____

_____

_____

What are you willing to let go of and lay at Jesus's feet today?

_____

_____

_____

_____

_____

My Journal Through Grief

ONE STORM AFTER ANOTHER

Journal Entry

March 2020

Last night my two dogs wanted to sleep right next to me. Basically, on top of me. There was a huge lightning storm. They were shaking, and I just let them get under the covers with me and put my arm around them. That lightning wasn't going to bother them. It wasn't likely that it would come through the window. I didn't mind them cuddling.

Then, I was reminded I've just gotten out of the biggest storm of my life, just to be thrown right back into another huge storm before I could even rest. That's the key. Rest. This storm isn't going to interrupt my rest this time. God is okay with us cuddling Him through it. He's got His arms around us. Let Him do the protecting. He will calm the storm. The one around you and inside you. Trust Him. He's got the whole wide world in His hands!

What fear is the storm you're in causing?

_____

_____

_____

_____

_____

Crystal Pain

What does God's Word say about that fear?

_____

_____

_____

_____

_____

What is one active way that you can rest in God today?

_____

_____

_____

_____

_____

My Journal Through Grief

AN INHERITANCE OF WISDOM

Journal Entry
April 2020

This is a picture of my amazing husband, Nathan, battling brain cancer. After two months, his body had begun to shut down. He couldn't walk, could barely talk or swallow, and saw two of everything.

He continued to worship the Father, and in this picture, he's using the only limb that he could use at the time to type. You see, the word tells us to seek first the kingdom of God, and "all shall be given unto you."

My husband, though physically miserable, did just that. He was only concerned about everyone else during this time. He wasn't afraid of death; he knew his creator and had a close relationship with Him.

But he did want to make sure that the assignment God placed on his life was continued. He did want to make sure he left something of value to his family and friends. You see Nathan knew God's wisdom was more valuable than gold or silver. With the help of the Holy Spirit, Nathan poured out on paper the wisdom God had placed inside him. The last month and a half, as his body was beginning to shut down, he fought Satan's attacks by leaving a tangible copy of that wisdom.

Nathan typed two devotional books during the last month and a half of his life. They are divinely inspired by the Lord and will bless so many for years to come. I'm so honored to have called him my husband, my ever-inspiration. The most selfless man I've ever known.

Crystal Pain

I hope you are just as blessed as we are by his example.

Is there anything in your life now that is preventing you from being a witness to God?

_____
_____
_____
_____

Is there a step you can actively take to worship Him in that struggle?

_____
_____
_____
_____

My Journal Through Grief

REST FOR PREPARATION

Journal Entry

April 2020

I believe God is saying we are soon entering a time of rest. A Sabbath. A time just before harvest when we rest from all the work. A time of overwhelming peace. However, resting from work is secondary at this time. It is a time of submitting and surrendering to the awareness of His great holiness and thankfulness for all He's given us that takes importance.

Eyes will be opened to all He has done for His people, and praises will fill the air for all He's delivered them from. Those praises are solidifying the preparations for a harvest season.

Those called to the marketplace, those called outside the four walls, missionaries, and those called to the streets take this season very seriously. He's calling you. He's preparing you. Harvest is close by. Embrace this process. He will need you ready for the demand will be great.

He says, "Remember and know the love I have for you! It will be what carries you through any fire. Share from that place of vulnerability, free from selfish ambition but overflowing with my authentic love.

Crystal Pain

Can you remember a time when God showed up for you and delivered you from a great trial?

_____

_____

_____

_____

_____

What is preventing you from believing that He will do it again?

_____

_____

_____

_____

_____

Are you willing to release that fear to God and ask Him to carry it?

_____

_____

_____

_____

_____

My Journal Through Grief

ANGEL KISSES

Journal Entry

June 1, 2020

Today I was stopped by a young lady who complimented my necklace. I noticed she was wearing one similar. It was a coin like mine. I asked what it said on it. She said it was a gift from her grandma and was a French saying meaning, "I love you more today than yesterday and a little less than I will tomorrow."

I'm doing good lately, and I smiled because this was a saying that Nathan told me daily. What are the chances? It was like a kiss from heaven saying, "I see you, and I'm happy you're smiling again." Thanks, babe!

God is good!

Is there anything that constantly reminds you of something beautiful in your past life?

_____

_____

_____

_____

_____

Are you willing to thank God for that?

_____

_____

_____

_____

_____

Crystal Pain

What is one way you can step out in faith today, believing God for even more blessings to come?

_____

_____

_____

_____

_____

My Journal Through Grief

REACHING FOR INSTANT GRATIFICATION

Journal Entry

June 17th, 2020

Sometimes in the middle of a trial or while walking through the fire, we find ourselves tempted to question God. We may find ourselves entertaining thoughts or lifestyles of our past. Satan tempts us with those things we used to reach for in the past for instant gratification. It's important when these things happen, we notice them just as they are, a trap set before us. Remember, we are not of this world; we are righteous by faith. The shame of our weakness has no place in our hearts. Our flesh may fail, but God is forever our strength and portion. Praise God, for He is right there holding our hand, side by side, walking us through the flames. How blessed we are!

Is there an area where you find yourself seeking instant gratification?

_____

_____

_____

_____

_____

Crystal Pain

What are things you are believing in?

_____

_____

_____

_____

_____

What instant do you think God wants to replace with a permanent one?

_____

_____

_____

_____

_____

My Journal Through Grief

DON'T LOSE YOUR JOY

Journal Entry

July 25th, 2020

Each time I have gone to visit Mom at the hospital,l something complicated has happened. I've had times when I was in absolute ugly fits. But it's helped me understand the ins and outs of the hospital and given me confidence in maneuvering around inside it. Today I ran into a lady who was frazzled. She was headed to pick up her husband, who was having a brain aneurysm. That happened to be the same thing that happened to Mom five days ago.

I told her, confidently and with a bubbly attitude, to "follow me." I walked with her to the SICU. I knew exactly where she needed to go.

I then ran back into her when we were leaving and walked with her out to the parking garage. I asked if I could pray for her. Afterward, she said, "You're a real joy. You've been a true witness to me."

I say this all because earlier this week, I lost my joy because of the complications. God used those trials, though. I was able to recognize that same fear in this woman because I had experienced it. I was able to help her because of it. Another amazing thing is that before Nathan died, he told me, "Don't lose your joy. It's your witness." That was the exact thing this woman told me.

It's okay to just be! It's ok if you mess up and don't always walk in peace. God will not punish you! If you stay focused on Him, He will even use you. If He can use a

Crystal Pain

messed up, high-strung woman like me. He can use you!

What are the areas or times you have lost your joy?

_____

_____

_____

_____

_____

Can you believe that God will use these areas to grow you?

_____

_____

_____

_____

_____

Is there someone today that might be going through something you have already walked through?

_____

_____

_____

_____

_____

My Journal Through Grief

DON'T BACK DOWN—GOD'S UNDISTORTED PLAN

Journal Entry

August 14th, 2020

This is a season God is going to expedite the process of walking through doors of favor and opportunity. We are called to be the light in the darkness. He only needs us to BE. It's time to speak over our given areas of influence and claim territory for His kingdom. That may be your home, land, investments, or businesses. Whatever atmosphere you're called to, come into agreement with God's Word and light it up! Favor, joy, and the abundant increase will be a witness and your light in this dark hour! It's time! Time to shine and lay down selfish motivation and a work-driven mindset. Partner with Him and allow His effortless power to flow through you. Brush off guilt and unworthiness! He is going to use you in areas you're not naturally good at. Step in to operating out of pure grace! All of Him, none of us! THIS IS NOT A TIME TO BACK DOWN!

Can you name at least one area in your life that you have influenced?

_____

_____

_____

_____

_____

Crystal Pain

Have you been motivated by selfish ambition in this area?

_____

_____

_____

_____

_____

Can you believe God for the increase in this influence?

_____

_____

_____

_____

_____

My Journal Through Grief

EARLY DETECTION OF SPIRITUAL WARFARE BIRTHED IN PRIDE

Journal Entry

September 2020

I feel in my spirit that there has been an attack by two specific spirits. There are many who have experienced great loss this year and have entered great grieving. Maybe you have lost your spouse, your mother or father, maybe you lost a child or experienced a miscarriage, maybe you had someone move away or move yourself. Maybe you have lost your job or suffered a divorce. Possibly the changes in the world lately due to the pandemic have caused grieving. These have been traumatic events that have brought you into a place of great grieving; you are grieving a life you once knew. You are in a place of great vulnerability.

Moving forward has been difficult, and the Lord has revealed to me two specific spirits that have attacked in this dry area you have found yourself!

Satan lurks in the dry areas of our lives, looking to devour what he feels are the weak. There has been a partnership of two spirits that resemble narcissistic personality traits. These two spirits are the Leviathan Spirit working with the Jezebel's spirit.

Jezebel has brought with her a seduction, making you feel as if you are being drawn into and entertaining a life of sin that you no longer participate in. It's making you

Crystal Pain

believe the old man within you is rising up. This man is dead! God created you NEW when you were adopted into His family. There is no old man. This is a lie of the enemy. Jezebel is controlling. She has used either someone in your life to control you or made you believe you need to control your life by going to extreme measures, releasing a strong sense of anxiety. She has made you self-reflect and hates who you are, even questioning your value and even dealing with suicidal thoughts.

She is under a ruling partnership of Leviathan. Which is Operating as a twisting suffocating spirit. Taking words spoken between you and others and twisting them causes people to hear things that are not actually being said. Otherwise known as gas lighting. You may even start believing horrible things about yourself and find yourself apologizing for things you never even entertained before.

Leviathan has a strong ego and has used others to make us question our own value and stripped us of even thinking we have anything to offer. It's making us question who we are and what our purpose is.

The way we break free from these spirits is not by rebuking them but rather by ridding ourselves of anything we may have in common with them. Stripping them of their power by using the gifts God has freely given us.

We renounce the spirits of pride, control, unworthiness, strife, doubt, and suicide. And repent of partnering with them.

We break off these things in Jesus' name and...

We finally rejoice and worship Him for His authority given to us and for the awareness of the schemes of the enemy. What has been in darkness remains under the control

My Journal Through Grief

of darkness, but those things brought to light have His healing freeing power shined on them! Thank you, Father, for your freedom! Thank you, Father, for bringing things to light!

Have you recognized any of these attacks?

_____

_____

_____

_____

_____

Are you willing to ask forgiveness for partnering with them?

_____

_____

_____

_____

_____

Crystal Pain

ANNIVERSARY OF THE DIAGNOSIS

Journal Entry

September 2, 2020

This time a year ago, we found out Nathan had an incurable inoperable brain tumor. As I read through my Bible, I see battle cries. I see us standing on His Word. I feel the battle wounds.

I have a choice.

1. To believe everything in here is a lie.
2. We didn't have enough faith.
3. God's ways are higher, and sometimes, there are mysteries we won't understand until we reach the other side.

We chose #3. Because no matter what, my God is good! We are in another battle now with our country. Let's keep standing!

What areas have you questioned God's truth?

_____

_____

_____

_____

_____

My Journal Through Grief

Have you questioned your own faith in any areas?

_____

_____

_____

_____

_____

Can you find the strength to ask God to carry these questions for you?

_____

_____

_____

_____

_____

Crystal Pain

THE FIRST LESSONS LEARNED

Journal Entry
October 16th, 2020

I reflected on the last time I laid next to my biggest blessing, my gift from God. It was right after he passed, and I climbed into the hospice bed with him. I know many have lost loved ones this year. I wanted to share a few things that I've learned over the last eight months in hopes of maybe helping someone walking through the biggest trial you've ever faced, the shattering of loss and grief.

1. Our ultimate goal in life is to make it to heaven and somehow help as many people as possible along the way. To help them encounter Jesus and experience His overwhelming love. My husband did this, and through his books, he continues this assignment. He was promoted early to our life goal. We aren't on this earth for pleasure and selfish gain. Although God often blesses us with many treasures.

2. God draws close to the broken-hearted, and during this time, I know Nathan was experiencing Jesus's fully manifested presence. We could say how did he choose to leave us and go with Jesus? But who wouldn't? What would it be like to be in Jesus's presence? What would it be like to feel his powerfully overwhelming love? Wow!

3. There's a bigger picture that we will never truly understand until we cross over ourselves. We won't truly understand why healing didn't manifest, but I know it's God's will for us to live long, prosperous lives. God is

My Journal Through Grief

GOOD. Always!

4. I wasn't always the best wife. I messed up a lot, had pride, a temper, etc. But because of losing my best friend and walking through this guilt, I choose to be better in this next chapter. He'd want me to be. Because of Nathan, I'll recognize these and choose to correct them or see the lack of significance in acting the way I did. In some strange way, through the pain of Nathan's death, he will help bring freedom from old ways in me. He was always so selfless and giving.

5. Faith is not always winning a battle. Faith is standing and fighting for your beliefs until the very end. Nathan was the biggest warrior I've ever met. He deserves a Purple Heart of Faith! He won, even when Satan whispered differently. He's now fighting for us all beside Jesus. We will experience the favor that He's sending down on us if we choose to recognize and receive it.

6. The biggest weapon of warfare is the sacrifice of Praise. Nathan allowed us access to this weapon. I will praise the name of Jesus even on the most painful days! Slapping Satan in his face each time.

Can you find at least one thing to praise God for today?

_____

_____

_____

_____

_____

Crystal Pain

What is one thing you can forgive yourself for?

_____

_____

_____

_____

_____

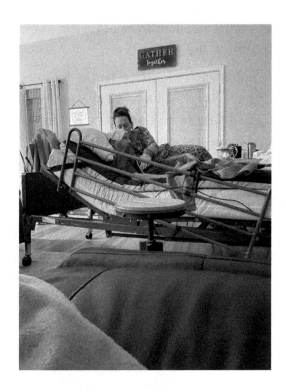

My Journal Through Grief

FEEL THE EMOTIONS

Journal Entry

November 8, 2020

I got up and went hunting this morning. I decided to sit on Nathan's stand this morning. I felt like I needed some God and nature time. I received a text from a friend who was walking out on my journey. She said, "Part of the healing process is letting ourselves travel down memory lane and shed tears over our losses that were and will now be without our soul mates."

I'm learning to smile through tears! This was hard! But it's going to be okay! The future will be bright! It's ok to allow yourself to feel the emotions.

Have you been shoving your emotions down?

_____

_____

_____

_____

_____

Is there one area you are willing to give yourself fifteen minutes to feel the pain?

_____

_____

_____

_____

_____

Crystal Pain

Can you invite God into that pain with you?

_____

_____

_____

_____

_____

My Journal Through Grief

EMBRACING A NEW CHAPTER

Journal Entry

January 1, 2021

Two thousand and twenty taught me life is short. It taught me balance and to set goals. However, it also taught me to live life without striving in between the progress markers. It taught me to seek God for his relationship, wisdom, and affirmation. This is done not to get what we want but to see what He's already given us. Two thousand and twenty taught me that love is the most important power and force in this world. We give and feel it every chance you get! It taught me that if you work on yourself and allow yourself to mold into who you are naturally, you attract the most authentic things that fit into your life best. Those things will be the biggest blessings. It showed me that there is a bigger picture and to not focus on those times, you color outside the lines.

Most of all, God showed me that He's a God of continuous blessing and will bring people into my life that line up with these newfound truths! I'm so thankful for the loved ones who've both come into my life this year and the old relationships that have blossomed. Here's to embracing a new chapter while treasuring the past one.

Crystal Pain

Is there an area where you have been striving in between?

_____

_____

_____

_____

What have you been holding onto that is preventing you from seeing the bigger picture?

_____

_____

_____

_____

Is there a place God has already brought wisdom out of the wounds?

_____

_____

_____

_____

My Journal Through Grief

YEAR TWO

Crystal Pain

FEAR BIRTHS HATE

Journal Entry

January 6, 2021

A time of metamorphosis is taking place for many. A stripping away of the old and transforming into a new being. Temptation to grab hold of the old is strong but focus on building up the new. For the scars of your sins could be the very ropes that tie you up. God is calling many to fly, like a butterfly stretching its new wings. The pains are being used to strengthen you for your next assignment. Do not rush them, medicate, or mask the process. Let joy and love rule your heart during this time. The enemy wants to cause divisions between God's people through confusion and unsteadiness. Walk only on His solid foundation found in the truth of His Word. It's the distortion of these truths that will knock you off the path of solid ground. Be alert, but don't let fear plant hate in your heart. Hate births evil. Guard your hearts, fill them with trust in all he's promised.

These truths will be a beam of light, a witness to others, and a guide to discovering new depths of freedom. He desires to bring true freedom!

My Journal Through Grief

Can you see an area that God has strengthened you in your journey?

Is there an area in your life where you can recognize a distortion in God's truth?

Are there areas in your heart that have been left unguarded?

Crystal Pain

RUNNING FROM ANXIETY

Journal Entry

March 6, 2021

Many might not know, but I've been dealing with EX-TREME anxiety. One of my coping mechanisms is jogging. It reminds me somehow that if I die to the cries of my flesh telling me to stop and not reach my mileage goal, it's the same for the cries in my soul (mind, will, and emotions) filling with lies trying to prevent me from moving forward.

Today, I ran into two dogs. A great Pyrenees and then a pitbull. I didn't show fear and just spoke to them in a calm voice. I understood they were territorial, and I was approaching their property. Both times they stopped barking and coming toward me after I passed their land.

I learned four things through this experience today.

1. Anxiety is just the enemy barking at you, threatened by you. Satan thinks you're going to take territory he's claiming for himself.

2. God's given us authority and dominion over all things. Your words have power. Remember to speak to your mountains. Not out of fear but confident in knowing your authority.

3. Dying to flesh can hurt and be uncomfortable, but most of that is lies. You can push past and do more than you realize. Keep moving forward.

4. It's okay if you have something attack you. It's okay to stop and handle the situation. Just get back on track and finish the race.

My Journal Through Grief

If you deal with anxiety, you're not alone. I'm thankful for those in my life who don't give up on me.

Are there any areas in your life that you recognize the enemy causing you anxiety?

_____

_____

_____

_____

_____

Are these areas that you trust God to bring freedom in?

_____

_____

_____

_____

_____

What's one truth you can speak into the fears you have regarding these areas?

_____

_____

_____

_____

_____

Crystal Pain

ESSENTIAL BREEDING HENS

Journal Entry

April 2nd, 2021

Turkey season is around the corner. It makes me a little emotional. Nathan would be out scouting, seeing where they were roosting, anxiously getting his camo and gear ready.

Today, I got overwhelmed with a bunch of things that have been on my plate lately. I really missed Nathan. Over the years, he learned the warning signs I displayed right before anxiety hit and somehow always knew exactly what I needed. He always knew exactly what to say in his special way.

I started thinking about us hunting turkey together. Then, I thought about how no one ever takes a hen (female). Did you know in some states, it's illegal?

They consider the hens that make it through the fall and winter essential to future generations as far as breeding successful broods goes.

This really spoke to me. There are a lot of people right now feeling like, or currently walking through, what feels like, the dead of winter. It's bitter and cold and looks like there is no end in sight. I really feel like it's those people God is saying, "You're going to come out an essential part of my kingdom, something highly desired to help successfully grow the church."

I felt uplifted, protected, needed, and energized. Just like Nathan telling me one of his stories with a beautiful message about God's grace packaged inside. I love how God

My Journal Through Grief

talked to me in a way that felt just like Nathan. I sure miss him, but I know he is always with me.

Do you feel like you've experienced a battle that others around you don't understand?

_____

_____

_____

_____

_____

Can you see a way you can be used to shed light on this battle?

_____

_____

_____

_____

_____

Name one thing today that you can actively do to speak on this.

_____

_____

_____

_____

_____

Crystal Pain

DISTORTED BODY IMAGE

Journal Entry

April 21st, 2021

These mannequins need a cheeseburger! One thing I absolutely hate about the women's retail industry is the striving to be super skinny. Many of you know my high school years and much of college were filled with striving to "look" perfect. I was perceived as an athlete, dedicated to working hard to be the best. In reality, I was chasing an image. I'd placed a man's opinion of me higher than anything and soon found an eating disorder controlling my life. I'd even gotten too weak to run track. One time, I even passed out on the track due to a lack of nutrition. I took a good thing and distorted it, and used it for vanity.

Our spiritual walk can be the same. Paul tells us in 1 Corinthians that an athlete will be disciplined in every way. But they are practicing winning an award that will amount to nothing. He goes on to say, as children of God, our reward is eternal. But if our motive isn't rooted in God. If our motive is distorted toward pleasing man, for image, for affirmation told us by man, you'll see the effects in your physical body. You'll get worn down, exhausted even. You must feed your spirit the proper nutrition. And that can ONLY come from intimacy with the one and only GIVER of the EVERLASTING reward.

Are there any areas that you once were strong that you now find difficult?

_____
_____
_____
_____

Has your motivation been distorted by anything?

_____
_____
_____
_____

What area in your life can you recognize you haven't turned over to God's control?

_____
_____
_____
_____

Crystal Pain

TRANSITION TEAM

Journal Entry

May 4th, 2021

Lately, I've been feeling God nudge me into a transitional season. It's made me anxious because I can't see the next step. I felt like I was stuck. I read Colossians and wanted to share. While Paul was "stuck" in prison, he wrote about loving people, prayer, and the partnerships/relationships he'd developed.

Sometimes our first steps in transition have more to do with preparation than plowing new ground. Preparing our hearts, remembering to let love flow, and keeping our eyes on Him through prayer. Paul surrounded himself with these four types of partnerships.

1. An intercessor—someone who intervenes on behalf of another through prayer. We all need backing like this.

2. A comforter and encourager—someone who never gives up on us and sees our strengths

3. A healer/counselor—those who give solid, godly advice and mentor us through rough times

4. Friends—people who stand with us in the fire.

I pray each person that is walking through a transitional season finds their team. That their eyes are open to see their tribe. New seasons aren't always easy, but being surrounded by the right people truly is the catapult!

My Journal Through Grief

Can you think of anyone in your life that could fill these roles for you?

_____

_____

_____

_____

_____

Can you actively step out and be in any of these roles for others?

_____

_____

_____

_____

_____

Crystal Pain

UNRECOGNIZABLE

Journal Entry

May 26th, 2021

When I looked at these two photos, I didn't recognize either one of these ladies. One was me a little over a year ago, and one was me today. But after looking closer, I realized my circumstances have changed, my life looks entirely different, and my views have slightly changed. BUT deep down in my core...I'm still the same.

If you find yourself in a season of change and maybe unsure of who you are anymore, just look deep down inside. Those things that make you filled with passion, joy, hope, or even anger, that's who you are. I've had great guidance from huge staples in my life to help me see those things that make me, me. Hold on to those gifts God gave you, and you'll never lose yourself.

Maybe you love organizing, maybe it's learning new things or studying things in depth, maybe you love serving others, maybe you're a great listener, or maybe you're a mother to others. Whatever it is, don't overlook the significance of the simplicity of what makes you... you! Here's to change while remaining the same!

What makes you filled with passion?

_____

_____

_____

_____

_____

Who can you go to in your life and ask them what your strengths are?

_____
_____
_____
_____

What do you recognize as one of your strengths?

_____
_____
_____
_____

Crystal Pain

YOU'RE GOING TO BE OKAY

Journal Entry

June 6th, 2021

I've been struggling lately, so I decided to go hiking alone to clear my head. The trails were muddy and slick. I got lost once (I have no sense of direction), so I decided to turn around and retrace my steps. I started crying, asking God, why I feel so lost? I always run backward.

He gently reminded me it's okay to retrace your steps. It's okay to see what you may have missed or overlooked. It's okay to see the areas you flew past that needed to be visited and touched.

I noticed on the way back there was a pier overlooking the beautiful lake. It was a gorgeous resting place. I thought, *Even though the trail was slick, rocky, and muddy, I always found a solid rock to place my foot. Or there was a strong branch to reach out and hold.*

Then, on my playlist, Jenn Johnson's song "You're Going to Be Okay" came on. This song speaks about keeping your focus on God and just taking life one step at a time. In that moment, it was God's little way of confirming to me that He's walking with me. I'm not alone, and He will guide my each step. Everything is going to be okay.

My Journal Through Grief

Name one time that you saw God show up for you.

_____

_____

_____

_____

_____

Name a time when someone else showed up for you.

_____

_____

_____

_____

_____

Name a time that you showed up for someone else.

_____

_____

_____

_____

_____

Crystal Pain

SLOWING DOWN DURING THE RACE

Journal Entry

June 27, 2021

During my morning run, the first two miles, I had the wind at my back. But on the way back, it was slowing me down big time. I was disappointed. Then I was reminded of Rayelyn (my daughter) when she ran cross country. At one meeting, she almost came in last, which wasn't like her (she's pretty fast). When I asked her what happened, she said she stopped to pray for a girl that was cramping up.

Sometimes in this life, we've got to take our focus off our accomplishments and those things the world tells us are most important. We must embrace the winds of change, and push through, knowing it's strengthening us to become better. Slowing down during difficult times for yourself and others in the race you've been giving isn't bad.

> *I just want to obey all you ask of me. So, teach me, Lord, for you are my God. Your gracious Spirit is all I need, so lead me on good paths that are pleasing to you, my one and only God!*
>
> **–Psalms 143:10 TPT**

My Journal Through Grief

Can you think of a time that you should have stopped for someone else on your journey?

_____

_____

_____

_____

_____

Can you think of a time that you should have stopped for yourself along your journey?

_____

_____

_____

_____

_____

Crystal Pain

WISDOM COMES FROM DEATH

Journal Entry

September 9th, 2021

Wisdom is KIND and CONSIDERATE of others. James 3 tells us that you can't operate out of true wisdom with selfishness in your heart. To gain true wisdom, you must die to yourself. This can be very painful. It can look like laying your dreams, desires, or personal goals at God's feet. Trading your simple thoughts for the revelation of knowledge of God can be a painful process, one that takes courage and boldness. I know because my whole life started about two years ago.

By keeping your focus on His promises. You see, we aren't returning them; we are receiving a new perspective on them. Exchanging them for His wisdom and acquiring this means we are gaining the keys to a long life where each year is more fruitful than the next. That's God's heart toward us!

I pray I'm always able to choose kindness, consideration of others, peace, and a teachable spirit OVER fear, bitterness, jealousy, or self-righteousness. God tells us these are the characteristics in which His wisdom flows.

My Journal Through Grief

Is there a dream, desire, or goal you have had to let go of?

What made this hurt the most?

Have you ever chosen bitterness, fear, or any other negative emotion over operating out of the fruit of the spirit?

Do you think God can bless you with a dream again?

Crystal Pain

DROP TO YOUR KNEES

Journal Entry

October 16th, 2021

I was visiting my mom in Iowa the week after my dad died. Mom was finally able to take a nap, so I decided to go for a jog around her neighborhood. At about the first-mile mark, I had three huge dogs come after me. Terrified, I just dropped to my knees in the street and lay down. The biggest one got inches from my face and turned around. The others followed his lead.

Life can feel like this like you're being attacked from all different angles. But what I saw was that one of the most powerful things we can do is drop to our knees. It's not submitting to the negative things; it's recognizing when we, in our own power, can't do anything. It's when we say, "God, I can't, but you can." It's in total surrender to Him that we see His protection, His provision, and His covering.

I got back up and finished my run! Why? Because I'm not alone in the race…neither are you!

Can you describe a time when you became aware that you could do nothing to change your circumstances?

_____

_____

_____

_____

_____

My Journal Through Grief

Are you willing to drop down in humility and trust God to help?

_____

_____

_____

_____

_____

Will you finish the race ahead of you?

_____

_____

_____

_____

_____

Crystal Pain

THE ORDINARY SPARROW

Journal Entry

October 18th, 2021

I think, in traumatic times, it's natural to look for signs of guidance. An extraordinary way God might communicate to you. You reach for anything to bring you strength.

Flying to my mom after Daddy's passing, there was a little sparrow walking around inside the airport lobby. To be honest, it's just an ordinary, not-so-pretty bird. Everyone loved it, though. It really was making everyone smile and laugh as they fed it. When I got to Mom's house, I was filling up their bird feeders, and a ton of sparrows came in. Mom said they are always around.

I felt like God was saying, "I'm in the everyday, the ordinary, the not-so-pretty, and even in the things people see as insignificant. If you don't lose focus and appreciate each day as a gift, you'll find joy and smile. I'm engulfed in all aspects of your life."

I pray I will never forget the significance of the simplicity of life!

What is one time you saw God show up in the everyday routines of life?

_____

_____

_____

_____

My Journal Through Grief

Is there anything in your life that you need to simplify your viewpoint?

Can you trust God is weaving every aspect of your life together?

My Journal Through Grief

YEAR THREE

Crystal Pain

LET GO OF CONTROL, GRAB HIS HAND

Journal Entry

January 3rd, 2022

I've had severe anxiety through December with tons of fiery paths to travel. In my prayers tonight, I mostly listened. This was what I heard God saying....

Release those things that are no longer important to you. I'm not pouring supply into those things anymore. You've sensed this shift, and though it's made you uneasy and your steps shaky, you've not let go of My hand. And I have not let go of yours. Giving up your right to understand is not an act of foolishness. I see your surrender and total dependence on Me. It's okay to feel the fear surrounding you; however, be careful not to partner with it. Acknowledge it, then close your eyes and let Me guide you. Don't be led or distracted by your carnal senses. I'm guiding you. I'm using these obstacles and hurdles to prepare you for what lies ahead. You prayed for strength and had a quick but packed session on control. When you control your life with faith and not fear, anxiety loses its grip. Those things gained in faith will only be maintained by faith. You, in and through your own ability, can do nothing. Lean into My grace. Remember My love for you and My plans to bring you hope, prosperity, and abundant blessings. Standing at the foot of a mountain blazing with fire, I will speak to you with guidance, protection, and favor. Don't let go, don't give up. I'm here, always. Speak to the mountains and remember the authority I've given you. All will be for My glory! I believe in you. Now trust Me.

My Journal Through Grief

Are you holding on to anything that you are not seeing God's fruit flow out of?

_____

_____

_____

_____

_____

What is one area you stopped holding God's hand in?

_____

_____

_____

_____

_____

What mountain is in front of you that you believe God to equip you in climbing?

_____

_____

_____

_____

_____

Crystal Pain

WHY ARE THINGS TAKING SO LONG?

Journal Entry

January 19th, 2022

This week I've had multiple things happening that felt like Satan was poking me in my chest, trying to get a reaction out of me. Okay, he might have gotten one a few times. But today, while driving, I heard the words echo through my head "Success is a mindset, not a position or title."

As many know, a lot has changed in my life in a little time, and with so much horizontally looking unfamiliar, it's easy to forget to look vertically. Looking vertically (to God) is where we see our firm foundation, our lifeline, our peace, our protection, and our source of everything needed. It's where we find our identity and who we are. Our circumstances can change, BUT nothing can change who God is. Who He is to us, through us, and for us remains consistent.

So many times, we forget about how much God loves EVERYONE involved in a situation and wants to bless them just as much. We focus on "why things are taking too long" or "this doesn't look like I thought." We forget God's working out a much bigger picture than we see on the one puzzle piece we've been given. Be patient and rest in the process.

I prayed for God to open my eyes to see and only focus on His movements. I pray for Him to send angels around my family and friends to stop anything that wasn't from

My Journal Through Grief

Him from affecting their lives. I pray that we all rest, knowing He is with us always. His grace is freely given, and mercy is overflowing. Let Him hold you. Just surrender and fall into His love.

It's a sweet place to be. In Him, there is true success. The battlefield to obtaining it is often in our mindset.

Is there a place in your life where you are seeking guidance from a horizontal viewpoint?

_____

_____

_____

_____

_____

Is there a place in your life where you have only been concerned with how it affects you and not others?

_____

_____

_____

_____

_____

Crystal Pain

DON'T BE A PUPPET

Journal Entry

January 29th, 2022

The enemy cannot read your thoughts but will try to influence them. Why? Because he knows if he gets your thinking corrupted, soon your speech will follow. Again, why does this matter?

God's power flows through His children, and He has entrusted it to us. We've been told we will give an account for every careless word we speak (Matthew 12:36).

He intended our words to bring life. He tells us our words have the ability to turn away wrath. They bring life, health, healing, and satisfaction.

We are also warned that hateful lies we speak can be like hitting someone with an ax (oh, my goodness)! And they also carry with them the law of attraction.

Don't let the enemy use you like a puppet master. See, Satan doesn't have the power to create. He only distorts and uses what God has already created. If he can influence your thought, ultimately gaining access to your speech, then he will use you to create and attract all kinds of negativity in your life.

Just something I've been really trying to be conscious of lately. I've been trying to renew my mind/thoughts daily by submitting them to God. Or, like my momma always told me, "You reap what you sow"!

Do not conform to the pattern of this world but be transformed by the renewing of your mind. Then you will be able to test and approve what God's

My Journal Through Grief

will is—his good, pleasing, and perfect will.

Romans 12:2 NIV

Is there anything you find yourself repeating that is not lining up with God's promise over your life?

_____

_____

_____

_____

_____

Have you said anything about anyone that you wouldn't say to their face?

_____

_____

_____

_____

_____

What is one blessing you are willing to commit to speaking out loud every day for this week?

_____

_____

_____

_____

_____

Crystal Pain

MASSAGING OUT PRIDE

Journal Entry

February 27th, 2022

I went for a massage this weekend. Before we got there, I told my friend, "I hope this lady doesn't treat me like a child." They told her beforehand not to go easy on me. That she did not!

This lady showed no mercy! At one point, she jumped on top of me. Y'all, I'm not a very big human! I got scared! Every part of my body she pushed on was screaming. My back, arms, and legs were in pain! I knew I had a lot of knots that needed to be worked out, so I was determined to suffer through it. At one point, though, I prayed (like literally PRAYED) God, this hurts! Why does everything hurt?

HE replied.

That's what control does to your body. You've been carrying things I never intended you to carry. You've picked back up things you once laid at My feet. One sight at a storm, and you run for cover. You've forgotten I'm the source of everything you've ever held. I'm more than capable of giving you everything you want. You're just not remembering that My best for you might not look or happen like you think. You've been trying to control and hold on to things in your own power. I've been trying My best to shake your hands free of things. I, in My power, want to bless you. I need you to trust Me again. With EVERY part of your life, trust Me. Let Me love you!

Sometimes in life, we can put walls up to protect us, especially when we've been through trauma. One of those walls is extreme independence. Although being independent isn't bad, be careful that by not needing any help,

My Journal Through Grief

you don't put up a wall that's keeping God out, too. God does not want you to partner with Him because He thinks you're weak. He's asking you to take His yoke because He knows your potential, and with His guidance, you'll become truly strong. Fear, doubt, and anxiety are often rooted in self-focus. Pride is a strong, painful knot to massage out. Stay humble and alert! God will reveal the enemy's scheme. Just spend some time with Him.

Have you been trying to control anything in your life?

_____

_____

_____

_____

_____

Is there an area within your body that is being affected by stress?

_____

_____

_____

_____

_____

What is one thing you are willing to resubmit to God and stop picking back up?

_____

_____

_____

_____

_____

Crystal Pain

DRINK MORE MILK

Journal Entry

March 10, 2022

I was at the gym yesterday and ran into a woman who I have always thought was absolutely beautiful, inside and out. She asked how I was. I told her, "Lots going on but just taking forever to manifest." She said, "God's timing!" And I replied, "He is in the waiting!" We laughed, and she continued to minister to me. It was a sweet time for me, feeling God's presence there in the gym. I told her at one point, I was not praying for strength anymore because with that prayer always comes developmental training. I just pray for energy now. I have been dealing with some health issues and even put myself on a liquid diet/fast to try to help.

As I was tanning there at the gym, I began to cry. I told God I was still mad at Him for making me walk this journey I have been on. That I know I have closed off part of my heart to Him throughout the past two years, but I want Him to come in and consume all of me again. I said, sorry, I have been holding anger there. I said, I look in the mirror now and don't recognize myself. Who am I? Who do you want me to be?

He told me just as I have been on a liquid diet for my physical health. I needed to return to a liquid diet for my spiritual health, too. Drink more of my milk is how He phrased it.

I have been meditating on this. Milk? What is milk? I have always been one that wants deep revelation of His Word. I wanted the meat of the word, something that takes a while for me to digest. But milk, I forget what milk is. God said, "Remember who I am before asking

248

My Journal Through Grief

who I created you to be. And drink YOUR milk!"

As I began to remember who He was, I started with His name. Jehovah Jireh, "the God who provides." Jehovah Rapha, "the God who heals." Yahweh Shalom, "The God of Peace. El Shaddai, "God Almighty." El Hayyim, "The living God." Yahweh Nissi, "The God who Protects." El Roi, "The God who Sees."

Such power is in His name! And HE LOVES US! HE CALLS US HIS! WOW! I had tears!

He said, "Now, what does your name mean?" I said, "Cecily Charlene means *little woman of blind faith.*" It clicked! Yes, Father, I commit! Thank you! I'm also thankful for my beautiful friend who took time out of her workout to minister to me.

Who is God to you?

_____

_____

_____

_____

_____

What is something about yourself that you know God gifted you with?

_____

_____

_____

_____

_____

Name one thing you are grateful for today.

_____

Crystal Pain

FACING FEARS

Journal Entry

March 15th, 2022

Sitting in outpatient pre-registration for some small testing at Durant Hospital, I heard in my head my daughter's comment about 2022 being a year of facing your fears. They led me down the hall to radiology, and I had a flash of walking this hall with Nathan from two years ago. I'm sitting in the same spot where we waited for imagining results. I thought this would destroy me.

I feel like many of us are coming into a season of full circle. Facing things you've avoided or experiencing circumstances you faced in the past. Standing in the face of fear! You might tremble still, BUT this time you're stronger. Things might shake, but I really think God wants to show you how strong you really have become with Him. When you've been stripped of everything you depended on outside of Him, there is really a peace. Knowing it's in His hands, He got you through so much and never failed you. He won't ever! He works all things together, and all it requires is us to love. I'm so thankful He's never left me or forsaken me! How do people live their lives without Him?

My Journal Through Grief

Is there an area in your life you are avoiding?

Can you recognize the areas that you have become dependent on things outside of God's power?

What is one step you can take to actively face these things with Him?

PRIDE IN LACK, WARNING TWO

Journal Entry

March 17th, 2022

Everywhere I look recently, I hear about others being abused by narcissistic people. I believe the spirit behind this is Leviathan and Jezebel. The root is pride. The Lord is shaking us free from trying to control our world in our own power. You're not that influential. It's His authority in us that sustains us. He's not causing things but allowing them. The "love" of money is a big door here. Don't find pride in things we possess versus who we carry in us. Next time you buy groceries or gas, check your heart. Are you feeling fear or thankful for provision to still be able to provide? Be careful what you're partnering with. There's a temptation to control rather than submit to God's provision in these times.

"Let my satisfaction be found in you. Don't let me be so rich that I don't need you or so poor that I have to resort to dishonesty just to make ends meet" (Proverbs 30:9).

"He is a wrap-around shield of protection for all his lovers who run to hide in him. Never add to his words, or he will have to rebuke you" (Proverbs 30:5–6).

He's got us. Trust the process! Sow a seed in faith. No better ground to reap a harvest than a sacrifice in faith. It also slaps the enemy in the face when you steward what God's given you for the betterment of others.

My Journal Through Grief

What area in your life has God provided for you throughout your struggles?

_____

_____

_____

_____

_____

Is there anything that you don't think you have enough to share?

_____

_____

_____

_____

_____

What's one scripture you can speak about that area that relates to abundance?

_____

_____

_____

_____

_____

Crystal Pain

EVALUATION IN THE TRANSITION

Journal Entry

April 5th, 2022

Many of us have found ourselves in a transitional season. Many are moving into an area outside their comfort zone. Maybe it's starting a new career, moving forward after experiencing great loss, or possibly even moving to a new city starting over. I know for me personally; it felt like a restart and caused me to go before God and reevaluate my life. I've asked Him to help me take inventory. What do I take into this new season, and what do I need to lay down? With this, what felt like a fresh new start has turned into a threshing floor. I've felt like I'm being beaten from all directions and run over by livestock. I've been financially, physically, and emotionally shaken.

I choose to trust Him in the trials and know through them, God is revealing strengths and blessings as well as pruning me of anything I previously carried that's not valuable. Feeling your flesh dying hurts badly. I've cried out to Him to redeem me!

The strange thing is, I feel myself being in a place much like Ruth. God is willing to redeem me, but there is always a time I have to stand before the things of the world and be okay with them deeming me unfavorable or unworthy of being redeemed. These are familiar lies I've heard in my head.

It's okay! No matter what Satan throws at us, God is always there to work everything out for good. He will not

My Journal Through Grief

only redeem us (just like Boaz did Ruth), but through the process, He will impart wisdom. No matter how painful death to the flesh is, choosing Him will always leave us with a greater harvest and enough to feed others. I pray I always choose wisely and receive confirmation of my choices. He will faithfully answer our cries.

Is there a place in your life where you found yourself outside your comfort zone?

_____

_____

_____

_____

_____

Are you willing to be viewed by others as unfavorable to conquer this lack of comfort?

_____

_____

_____

_____

_____

What is one way God promises to equip us?

_____

_____

_____

_____

_____

Crystal Pain

FIGHTING FROM A PLACE OF REST!

Journal Entry

April 12, 2022

During worship service, I had a vision. I saw a lioness ferociously fighting off a pack of what appeared to be hyenas. She was wounded, and the fur on her underbelly was blood-soaked. She never gave up but was growing extremely weary. Then, out of nowhere, a majestic Lion stepped in front of her and let out a ground-shaking roar. The pack of prey ran off. I heard the Lord say, "The battle is not yours to fight. You are a mighty warrior in my kingdom, but in this hour, I am revealing a new way. One done in rest."

I believe the Lord is speaking to many of us in this vision. If you are like me, there have been attacks coming from all directions. You've found yourself fearful of resting, maybe even losing physical sleep due to the unrelenting attacks. You have not given up and even continue to defend yourself, your family, and those things entrusted to you by God while feeling wounded and beaten up.

I asked God to show me how to rest when everything around me requires me to be actively involved in finding the solution. He led me to Psalm 4. Throughout this passage, the writer is being attacked and crying out to God. Repeatedly, it says, "Pause in His Presence prior to instruction on how to handle the situation." What stood out to me the most was God's instruction to offer a righteous sacrifice of trust and meditate on our sins and repent. He

My Journal Through Grief

took our focus off the attack and back onto our souls.

Then I was reminded that our battles are not in the flesh, but they are spiritual. I truly feel that many have been battling spiritual attacks with fleshly instincts. God sees our submission to Him (through trust) as a righteous sacrifice and our denying of flesh as an offering to Him that is holy. Our job is to rid ourselves of anything we have in common with the things attacking us. This is the only way they lose their grip on altering our peace and instilling chaos into our lives.

Take time to rest and search your soul. We cannot control the world around us, but we can control what we allow inside our hearts. Deny fleshly reactions, whether it is taking offense, becoming bitter, carrying unforgiveness, slander, blaming others, or fighting fire with fire. Also, don't fear pain. One of the biggest fears in life is pain. However, God is closest to us in times of pain. With pain comes birthing, breakthrough, guidance, humility, discipline, and growth.

He comes to fight our battles for us if we submit and get out of His way. We are called to release good into this world, and He is a hedge of protection around us from anything altering that good.

If we find ourselves facing anxiety, God releases peace. If we find ourselves facing hate, he releases love. If it's indiscipline, He releases self-control. If it's sorrow, He releases joy. Our job is just to choose our weapons wisely. One will invoke weariness, and the other rest. Release what has freely been given to you through God taking up residence inside you. I have several strongholds that need to be broken, but I want freedom. I want to learn to fight in rest!

Crystal Pain

How have you been fighting?

_____

_____

_____

_____

_____

What is one way you can use God's fruits to combat the attacks coming against you?

_____

_____

_____

_____

Name one way you can rest in God while there is an active battle going on around you.

_____

_____

_____

_____

_____

My Journal Through Grief

EDGE OF A CLIFF

Journal Entry

July 14, 2022

I've recently walked through a season of extreme pruning. Stripped! I've been walking a foggy path. I've been clinging to Jesus' hand because anytime I let go, I get turned around. It feels like I've come to a cliff, and there's nowhere to go.

I heard God (with confirmation) say jump. What if I fall? What if I can't soar and crash?

I heard the scripture echo through my head, anything you put your hand to, He will prosper. But I've seen this cliff before, and I failed.

God said, "Because you weren't prepared before, now is the right time." Now!

I have a feeling many are in a season of full circle. Encountering things they attempted in their past, seeing a type of *déjà vu* in their lives happening. Slightly different but still the same from years ago, maybe a dream from their past resurfacing. It's scary because it's a completely different world you're living in now.

God showed me that the time of plowing new ground, planting, germination, and pruning has been exhausting, but the harvest that stands before us is unlike anything we've ever seen. Then I feel like he said there's an emphasis on developing three types of people. Caretakers, gardeners, and teachers.

Caretakers: one who nurtures, brings unity to the home, imparts selflessness, and operates in healing.

Crystal Pain

Gardeners: one who recognizes and cultivates gifts within someone's inner being. They help deliver others by calling out the things that are unhealthy and fertilizing the things that need growth. They have strong discernment of good and evil.

Teachers: they reveal truths and have a way of breaking down complex ways into easy steps to follow. They equip, instruct, and train you in new thought processes.

If you're standing at a cliff, scared and carnally wanting to just give up, know He created you to fly! Surround yourself with people who will equip you in areas you feel weak. He will highlight them to you. But don't fear. Soar!

Where have you felt pruned?

_____

_____

_____

_____

_____

What do you believe God wants to replace those things with?

_____

_____

_____

_____

_____

My Journal Through Grief

Can you recognize any caretakers, gardeners, or teachers in your life?

Crystal Pain

THE ACCEPTANCE STAGE

Journal entry

July 16th, 2022

There's a stage in my grief walk called acceptance.

You accept they are gone. You'll miss them badly, but you have gone from disbelief and denial (mixed with rebellious disobedience). It kind of looks like: "No, I don't want life. I don't want to live the life you put before me since before I was born, "it's too hard without my partner."

Then you say, "Okay! I'll do it. I'll learn to love my life all over again." This new chapter you have for me. It feels lonely, but I accept it's my only option, and you've never failed me before. What's my new assignment?

#1. You must let go of former dreams as a couple. They won't work with just one of you. This hurts because there's a deeper awareness of your true loss. It's not just their absence but the secondary losses as well.

#2. Okay. What are my gifts? Naturally, given that it freely flows from me. Things that I don't realize don't come easy for everyone. Maybe it's things that even irritate me when others don't do them or walk in them correctly. Maybe things that aren't reflected in others' actions or emotions get under your skin.

#3. I know who I am again. Now let's learn your passions. Things that you like doing and feel joy in the planning, as much as even doing. The things that you want to talk about often and share with others. This is hard because you might find the things you used to do with your lost

My Journal Through Grief

loved one are too painful to do now. But you (with trial and error) develop those things that fit this new you perfectly.

#4. God, how can I use these things mixed with who I am to make a difference? God, give me a new vision.

#5. God starts preparing your path, planning every divine appointment and every act of favor. Simultaneously, God separates you so He can have your undivided attention as you focus on Him. He downloads wisdom, knowledge, understanding, counsel, might, and a fresh introduction to His spirit. You developed a new fear of God.

#6. God reveals a glimpse of your new vision. Why, only a glimpse? To keep you clinging to Him and developing your TRUST! This is a stance you take going forward. It's accompanied by the action of praise. Guard your heart here! The enemy didn't think you'd even make it here. He'll try and take you down with anything. Yes, even the old ways he used to (he's not creative).

Then you start thinking, *could this new vision be more blessed than even my former one?* I didn't say a bigger blessing, but more blessed! Will there be more blessings, more opportunities, more wisdom, more influence, and more understanding of how God moves? Will you get to see deeper into His heart and encounter His grace, provision, favor, covering, and stronger presence than ever before? Will you get to see and know Him more than ever? Will you truly know your rightful place as royalty?

I'll let you know one day!

Crystal Pain

Can you recognize any of these stages you've walked through?

_____

_____

_____

_____

_____

What area have you already gained wisdom and understanding?

_____

_____

_____

_____

_____

How can you share this with others?

_____

_____

_____

_____

_____

My Journal Through Grief

THE PATH OF PEACE

Journal Entry

July 23, 2022

My heart has been a little broken lately, so I decided to go hiking. This trail ends up overlooking the lake, and it's always a beautiful place for me to sit with God and pray. Before I started, I heard God remind me that He's always with me on the journey to my final destination. When I got to the end of this particular hiking trail, there was already a large group there. I was disappointed in not getting the opportunity to sit quietly with God, overlooking the beautiful lake but remembering God's words.

I briefly reflected on the great things I got to see on the trek. I remembered the people I stopped to talk with, the smell of camp food, and the laughter of kids around me. There was one point I came to a fork in the trail and wasn't sure which one to take. Turns out they both led to the same place (one was just more difficult than the other). I accidentally took the more difficult path. It guided me to a trail super close to a cliff. I was forced to watch my every step so I didn't slip. I realized difficult things strengthen us if we don't let them destroy us. They keep us focused and physically aware of our surroundings.

Just a few weeks ago, my foot was broken, and God healed it. I know He will heal my heart too. It just takes one step at a time.

I'm thankful that we can feel lonely, but we are never truly alone. It's all in what we choose to focus on. Joy is in the present and not just found at the end of the journey, and forward movement is the key.

Crystal Pain

Describe when you feel the most alone.

_____

_____

_____

_____

_____

Where have you recently found you were disappointed?

_____

_____

_____

_____

_____

Ask God to reveal where He was at that moment. Did God have a different plan you overlooked?

_____

_____

_____

_____

_____

My Journal Through Grief

SEEDS OF CONFUSION

Journal Entry

August 28th, 2022

I feel like this is the year of prodigals coming home! Their return will make you question their commitment and motive, but I believe God is saying to run and greet them with mercy.

At the same time, the enemy is sending out deception like never before. Wanting us to question God's powerful touch on these individuals.

Satan has been raising up false prophets and increasing accessibility to black magic and witchcraft. Curses disguised as truth. Playing on impatience and our fresh need for instant gratification vs. standing on faith and God's timing. Satan's strategy is to get us to receive distractions and therefore plant a seed of confusion. Making us question clarity on God's guidance that is being spoken over us. Putting multiple voices in our head and not being able to tell which voice is true.

Keep focused on God. His voice, His character, His principles, His love. Take intimate time with Him to not forget what the peace of His presence is. Intimate time without agenda to just let Him love on you. This will hold your discernment. He will release the truth.

And our assignment to both protect ourselves from being deceived and love His sheep will be fulfilled. Armor on, swords raised. We are growing our family!

Crystal Pain

Have you found yourself confused about beliefs you once were solid on?

_____

_____

_____

_____

_____

What caused this confusion?

_____

_____

_____

_____

_____

What does God's Word say about these?

_____

_____

_____

_____

_____

My Journal Through Grief

NOT DEFINED BY THIS

Journal Entry
September 23, 2022

I was talking with God this morning. They say when you experience great trials, you have three options. You can let it define you, let it destroy you, or let it strengthen you.

I WILL NOT BE DEFINED BY THIS! I always used to stand on my faith and say things like, "We won't accept this diagnosis...God says we are healed." Or "I don't want any title defining me but will find my identity in Christ. He says who He created me to be, He is whose promises I trust and stand on!"

Then I became a widow and then lost my dad back-to-back. I entered life with grief. Grief is like being diagnosed with an incurable disease. Most days, you feel good, but you'll have flare-ups that come out of nowhere that will knock you on your booty. Some might last a few hours, other days. They tell you, "You'll live with this for the rest of your life but will have medication for symptoms and therapy for your emotional needs." Hmmm!

I thought, *How do you do this? I don't have a reference point on this battlefield. It isn't like fighting a disease. I'd fight that with scripture and know it must go because, with God, all things are possible.* This is different.

Grief is like the amputation of a leg. You'll learn to walk again, and if you choose, life still turns out beautiful. Although you're always aware of that part being amputated. And sometimes, there are ghost pains.

Crystal Pain

I've found it's one day at a time, with a tribe surrounding you. It's God's love and giving your self-permission. Permission to feel and fall down. But never permission to stay down!

Grief isn't talked about much unless, of course, from a negative standpoint. However, positively, things are birthed inside you when experiencing it. New compassion as well as an intolerance for people living life in a purposeless manner. You gain an awareness of how a heart can have a piece cut out from it and yet continue to grow and experience new, exciting things at the same time. I wouldn't choose this journey for anyone. However, I know if God saw me strong enough to walk this path, I say yes then. Yes, to let grief strengthen me.

To anyone walking through a grief journey, remember, nothing can destroy you. You're a child of God. No one said the path would be easy. But usually, things are birthed with a lot of labor pain. This life is over in a blink. You have been given a first-hand glimpse into the deepest workings of the heart, those surrounding great LOVE and great HEARTACHE. Use that opportunity wisely. Everyone's experience is different, so don't depend solely on "walking the stages." Tap into the deep work going on in your heart. It can be messy, like an art studio while creating a piece of art or your kitchen while baking a new recipe. That's okay! Trust God, He's the creator and author, and He wants to birth beauty out of ashes. You are not alone, you are not misunderstood, and you are not damaged. That's a lie from Satan. You are being refined, equipped with new wisdom, and activated for something new. God's got you in His hands.

My Journal Through Grief

Have you found yourself down and unable to get back up?

_____

_____

_____

_____

_____

Do you believe that others need to understand your pain?

_____

_____

_____

_____

_____

What place are you willing to exchange being understood with gaining God's revelation knowledge?

_____

_____

_____

_____

_____

Crystal Pain

MOTIVATED BY LIES

Journal Entry

November 19th, 2022

Tonight, I was at the gym late. No one was there. I did thirty-five minutes of cardio, some weights and abs, and then left. What was my motivation? Good question! I'd love to say that it's because I really want to be healthy and take care of myself. BUT tonight, as I sat in the gym alone, I pondered this question.

I think a lot of times I listen to lies. The lies become my motivation. Some lies I think the enemy places in my head through others or society in general, and some I just tell myself. I tell myself I'm slaying demons of anxiety, taking it out on the weights. I tell myself, *if I don't look a certain way, no one will ever want me again (and I don't want to be alone).* I tell myself, *if I can lift more or run longer, I've accomplished something more than I once did, so it's making me a better person.*

By placing my worth in others' opinions (or my own) and not what God says of me, it's me idolizing something other than God. Isn't that a sin? (I'm open to correction here.)

God says that He uncovers our sins with His light, and we are to admit them and ask His forgiveness. By not admitting them, we make Jesus a liar in our eyes (1 John). The truth is no weapon formed against me can prosper. God is my provider, my comfort, my friend, and my protection, and true beauty comes from a gentle and peaceful spirit that is precious to God as well as recognized by others.

My Journal Through Grief

Can you share one lie that you are being motivated by?

_____

_____

_____

_____

_____

Have you placed your value in the hands of others in any area of your life?

_____

_____

_____

_____

_____

Who does God say you are?

_____

_____

_____

_____

_____

Crystal Pain

FRAMEWORK OF CHANGE

Journal Entry
November 28th, 2022

What God did in the past, he can do again. To be honest, God has transformed my life more than once. The first round of learning and pruning and dying to flesh hurt! I know, however, the season afterward, it was dreams coming true and physically experiencing good change. It was refreshing.

Yet, I fight a beast of monster called fear. It's the remembrance of the pain it took to obtain the dream. I don't know if I am strong enough to do it again.

Then, God reminds me. His change isn't temporal. His change is in your framework. One board is out of place, and you've become awakened (through your previous round) to recognize and fix the issue immediately to prevent future more aggressive pain. It's an awareness that won't truly ever leave you. You can try and ignore it, but you still know it's there.

He always changes us in a way that equips us to advance with ease and reliance on Him. The first round did hurt, your flesh was dying, and your foundation wasn't concrete. Change, His change doesn't always come cheap. But once you obtain it, it never loses its value.

My Journal Through Grief

What is one thing God has done for you?

_____

_____

_____

_____

Where is one area where God has positively changed you?

_____

_____

_____

_____

What is one piece of wisdom you've gained through struggles?

_____

_____

_____

_____

Crystal Pain

DELIVERY ROOM

Journal Entry

December 6th, 2022

A few days ago, we got to welcome my great-niece into the world. While we were there, the nurse was taking the sweet baby girl's blood. It was the most beautiful thing seeing my niece's and her husband's love for their little girl. As I saw a tear slide down my niece's cheek and heard the encouraging words her husband was speaking over their baby during this. It touched us all. We each had a reaction to just how precious this baby was. That room, for the brief moment I was in it, was the purest state of love I've felt in a long time.

I was reminded of something, too. So many are spiritually pregnant now and need to understand something. You should be aware of the atmosphere in your delivery room. What are you allowing in it? You want your newborn's entrance to be into an atmosphere of peace, love, and acceptance. The place where God's voice and perspective are seen is the clearest.

While many of you are entering this birthing season. Ask yourself if those you have surrounded around you are on the same vibration as what God is birthing through you. Just as you are instructed to guard your heart, it's time to prepare your delivery room! What you are bringing forth deserves the same purity that we encountered in my niece's room. Oh! How beautiful this little one is!

My Journal Through Grief

What does the atmosphere around you look like?

_____

_____

_____

_____

_____

Do you need to rid your surroundings of anything?

_____

_____

_____

_____

_____

What is one thing you can do today to prepare your atmosphere to bring forth something new?

_____

_____

_____

_____

_____

My Journal Through Grief

YEAR FOUR

Crystal Pain

CLEANSING SHOWERS

Journal Entry

January 7th, 2023

I've found that walking through extreme loss, as my heart was hurting, my first reaction was to cling to God! My heart was shattered multiple times over these past few years. It was a pain I masked often. Mainly, I just didn't want others to feel uncomfortable in my presence. Don't get me wrong. I did gain a lot of wisdom on the journey. For this, I'm thankful. You see, when you shatter a bone, the pain doesn't go away quickly. You often get medicine that stops it. Helping you relax and heal faster. When your heart is shattered, there's no medicine to stop that pain. My heart ached nonstop for months and off and on for years. The temptation is to grab a quick fix. I ended up picking up things from my past to soothe it. Recently I've purged my life of these things. My eyes were opened to the truth that I didn't NEED them. They just became a habit at that point.

Today, as I was scrubbing and cleaning my shower, I was thanking God for cleansing my soul of these patterns in my life (a second time), wondering why I so easily picked them back up in the first place. God showed me because they were attached to familiar spirits.

After losing so many things in such a short period of time, my life felt unrecognizable, and I was searching for anything that felt familiar. I knew the things my heart was aching for were gone forever. But Satan has a tricky way of putting counterfeits in your life. They first seem to soothe and comfort, but once we give these things access

My Journal Through Grief

to our lives, they open the door to our soul to allow the enemy in. I'm so thankful for God's cleansing power, His mercy and forgiveness, and His grace that is sufficient! The restart button has been pressed!

Is there anything in your life strictly because it feels familiar?

_____

_____

_____

_____

_____

Is this something that is bringing growth or hindrance?

_____

_____

_____

_____

_____

Do you have anything in your life that you need to hit the restart button on?

_____

_____

_____

_____

_____

Crystal Pain

FALSE START

Journal Entry

February 25th, 2023

If you know me, you know I'm a runner. God often speaks to me in track terms. Lately, I was bummed out and told God it feels like I'm set for the race and just get out of the blocks just to have a false start, over and over. Why?

Two days later, I was sitting across from a beautiful sister in Christ at lunch, and she (not knowing how God talks to me) said, "I see you down, ready for a race, but God is saying to get back on the sidelines. You need rest and conditioning." I was blown away.

You see, I've been dealing with a lot of exhaustion, fear, and shame lately. Striving to find myself and identify who I am. I went through a season of backsliding. I repented, and God has been walking me through some inner healing. Wearing the badge "prodigal" like a scarlet letter.

Today at the Women's Conference, one of the speakers invited us to pray over each other's feet; to release a new spring in our step. I looked down and saw (in my mind's eye) my track shoes on my feet. When I got home, I ran to my hope chest and found my old high school stuff. There they were!

I tried them on and saw the number 27. I wrote on them (my time in the 200-meter dash). I wrote it on there in school to keep me focused before each race.

Today, I looked up Psalm 27 and wept. Just like that race, our race in life requires our focus on God's love and word. I heard God speak, and I want to say this to EVERYONE

My Journal Through Grief

who's battling the shame of backsliding.

Welcome back!

Just because it's not time for your race doesn't mean you're still not on the team! Let God finish His work in you. Conditioning is just as important! He wants you to be healthy and whole to prevent injury again. He works everything together for good! Stop doubting!

> Move your heart closer and closer to God, and He will come even closer to you. But make sure you cleanse your life, you sinners, and keep your heart pure and stop doubting. Feel the pain of your sin, be sorrowful and weep! Let your joking around be turned into mourning and your joy into deep humiliation. Be willing to be made low before the Lord and he will exalt you!
>
> James (Jacob)

Is there anything that you feel you've tried to start that just won't get off the ground?

_____

_____

_____

_____

Have you questioned if you are worthy of being used by God?

_____

_____

_____

Crystal Pain

What lie are you still believing about yourself?

What does God's truth tell you about that area?

My Journal Through Grief

LEAD POISONING

Journal Entry

March 8, 2023

Some lead poisoning symptoms include learning disabilities, fatigue, hyperactivity or irritability, insomnia, headaches, and memory loss. It's interesting that something so poisonous is the same material used to create beautiful crystal glasses we use for fancy dinner parties. The higher the lead content, the greater the brilliance and clarity in such pieces. They say they have a distinct ring to them when tapped or struck.

I can't help but reflect on this season we are in. You can't get on social media without seeing something about healing, growing, or becoming the best version of yourself. It seems that we all are in a season of recognizing the poison in our lives and turning it into something that is beautiful. Something that we are proud to show off at a fancy engagement. I know that the season I have been walking through, I felt the poisonous effects. Like lead poison, I felt fatigued, insomnia, irritability, and growth/learning was difficult.

I read that before you use crystal drinking glasses, you are to soak them in vinegar for twenty-four hours. Vinegar! Wow! With Easter approaching, I was thrown into a vision of Jesus on the cross. Taking all our sins and iniquities upon Himself. Disfigured and beaten to a bloody pulp, He hung there. For us! They offered Him vinegar wine to drink. Did you know that it was customary to give those being crucified drugged wine (wine with myrrh)? It was used to help numb the senses during crucifixion.

Crystal Pain

Soldiers would also drink this same wine when they were injured or about to die. Jesus refused it the first time. He didn't partake of this numbing wine until He knew the work was finished.

I think back to the times this season when I have reached for something to numb the pain I was in. Crying out, "God, why have you forsaken me?" Not realizing that the poison that was rising out of me was not to trigger me into sin or helplessness. It was for me to recognize that Jesus had already done everything for me, and it is time for me to see these poisons in my life and place them under the purification process of Jesus's blood! It was because God wants to take me into a place in this coming season that when I encounter something that taps or strikes me, I let out a distinct sound, a kingdom ring. One that shifts the atmosphere and is pleasant to the ears.

They soak the glass for twenty-four hours. The number "twenty-four" represents authority, governmental perfection, and complete maturity. We can't expect to have this in our world today if we don't first submit to the purification process within us. I know when IT IS FINISHED, that fresh new wine is going to be wonderful at our fancy dinner party! A true feast!

My Journal Through Grief

Have you felt any of the effects of lead poisoning?

What areas of your life do you feel need to be revisited?

Are you willing to allow God to reveal His truth and accept healing in those areas before grabbing anything to numb the pain?

GIVE CREDIT WHERE CREDIT IS DUE

Citations:

"Inherited Family Trauma." Mark Wolynn, 25 Jan. 2022, https://markwolynn.com/inherited-family-trauma/.

Kingdon, Mackenzi. "The End of the Line: It's Time to Face the Pain." RESTORATION COUNSELING, RESTORATION COUNSELING, 16 Oct. 2018, https://www.restorationcounselingseattle.com/blog/the-end-of-the-line-its-time-to-face-the-pain.

Little, Becky. "The Seven Deadly Sins and Where They Came from." History.com, A&E Television Networks, 2021, https://www.history.com/news/seven-deadly-sins-origins.

Armstrong, Lee "The Right Questions? Discovering your Gifts, Talents, Purpose and Calling." 17 April 2022.

Breathitt, Barbie. "A-Z Dream Symbology Dictionary by Dr. Barbie L. Breathitt." 4 May, 2015.

Comer, J. M. (2021, September 28). Live No Lies: Recognize and Resist the Three Enemies That Sabotage Your Peace. WaterBrook.

Topher (n.d.). Topher. https://tophertown.com

Jeane Dixon | Kermit Zarley (patheos.com) www.patheos.com/blogs/kermitzarleyblog/2013/09/jeane-dixon/

Wright, H. W. (2009, February 1). A More Excellent Way: Be in Health.

A quote by Abraham Lincoln. (n.d.). Quote by Abraham Lincoln: "A House Divided Against Itself Cannot Stand." https://www.goodreads.com/quotes/8033-a-house-divided-against-itself-cannot-stand-i-believe-this

ABOUT THE AUTHOR

Cecily Williams grew up in the Bible Belt. She has worn many masks of success, but deep down often felt like a misfit. The obstacles she found herself encapsulated in birthed true compassion to help others. She has a desire to pinpoint and recognize the root causes of any bondage others find themselves facing and equip them with the tools needed to break free. Drawn to marketplace ministry, she uses her seer and prophetic anointing to encourage others to know they each walk with something beautifully their own. She believes God can and will use any struggle life throws at you by turning it into growth, wisdom, and a platform to reach others. Her life hasn't always been easy, faced with being a single mother and young widow brought its challenges. She found that true submission, humility, and devotion to God meant that she was never alone in the trials. Jesus became her best friend in the lonely times. He is the source of all the power needed to not just survive but to thrive.

Printed in the USA
CPSIA information can be obtained
at www.ICGtesting.com
LVHW020028310823
756763LV00003B/4